Identity and Data Security for Web Development
Best Practices

Jonathan LeBlanc and Tim Messerschmidt

Beijing · Boston · Farnham · Sebastopol · Tokyo

Identity and Data Security for Web Development

by Jonathan LeBlanc and Tim Messerschmidt

Printed in the United States of America.

Published by O'Reilly Media, Inc., 1005 Gravenstein Highway North, Sebastopol, CA 95472.

O'Reilly books may be purchased for educational, business, or sales promotional use. Online editions are also available for most titles (*http://safaribooksonline.com*). For more information, contact our corporate/institutional sales department: 800-998-9938 or *corporate@oreilly.com*.

Editor: Meg Foley	**Indexer:** WordCo Indexing Services, Inc.
Production Editor: Colleen Cole	**Interior Designer:** David Futato
Copyeditor: Kim Cofer	**Cover Designer:** Karen Montgomery
Proofreader: Sharon Wilkey	**Illustrator:** Rebecca Demarest

June 2016: First Edition

Revision History for the First Edition
2016-06-03: First Release

See *http://oreilly.com/catalog/errata.csp?isbn=9781491937013* for release details.

978-1-491-93701-3

[LSI]

Table of Contents

Preface

"Companies Lose $400 Billion to Hackers Each Year"[1]

—Inc. Magazine

A cybersecurity market report issued by Cybersecurity Ventures in Q4 of 2015 stated that cyber attacks are costing businesses between $400 and $500 billion a year.[2] In the same thread, IT security spending is due to increase by 4.7% in 2015 to $75.4 billion USD, with an estimate that the world will spend upward of $101 billion in information security in 2018, and grow to $170 billion in 2020. Therefore, a cybersecurity workforce shortage of 1.5 million people is projected by 2019, as demand is expected to rise to 6 million that year.

As web and application developers, designers, engineers, and creators, we are no longer living in an age where we can offload the knowledge of identity and data security to someone else. By not understanding how to properly obscure data in transmission, a web developer can unwittingly open up a security flaw on a site. A project manager can cause a major attack vector to open up in an application by not understanding that previously secure password algorithms have been shown to now include flaws, and by not prioritizing the work on rehashing the database of user records. It is now the business of every person working on a system to take part in ensuring that users and data are protected.

Despite this awareness, it seems like every week we have new cases of companies, from startups to massive corporations, losing privileged user information, credit card data, medical records, and many other pieces of information that they are entrusted to protect. It has come to light that many of these same organizations never took the time to encrypt data properly, storing everything in plain text, just waiting for some hacker to abuse it.

---

1 *http://www.inc.com/will-yakowicz/cyberattacks-cost-companies-400-billion-each-year.html*

2 *http://cybersecurityventures.com/cybersecurity-market-report*

The true problem is that hacking is no longer just the business of individuals wanting to prove that they can breach a system; it is now a realm of organized businesses, hacking for money or to damage the business.

This is where this text comes in. As we explore each chapter and concept, you'll learn how to plug holes in existing systems, protect against viable attack vectors, and work in environments that are sometimes naturally insecure. We'll look at concepts such as the following:

- Understanding the state of web and application security
- Building security password encryption, and combating password attack vectors
- Creating digital fingerprints to identify users through browser, device, and paired-device detection
- Building secure data transmission systems through OAuth and OpenID Connect
- Using alternate methods of identification for a second factor of authentication
- Hardening your web applications against attack
- Creating a secure data transmission system using SSL/TLS and synchronous and asynchronous cryptography

In the end, you'll have a comprehensive understanding of the current state of identity and data security, knowing how to protect yourself against potential attacks, and protect our users from having the data that they entrusted to you compromised.

Conventions Used in This Book

The following typographical conventions are used in this book:

Italic
> Indicates new terms, URLs, email addresses, filenames, and file extensions.

`Constant width`
> Used for program listings, as well as within paragraphs to refer to program elements such as variable or function names, databases, datatypes, environment variables, statements, and keywords.

`Constant width bold`
> Shows commands or other text that should be typed literally by the user.

`Constant width italic`
> Shows text that should be replaced with user-supplied values or by values determined by context.

This element signifies a tip or suggestion.

 This element signifies a general note.

 This element indicates a warning or caution.

Safari® Books Online

 *Safari Books Online* is an on-demand digital library that delivers expert content in both book and video form from the world's leading authors in technology and business.

Technology professionals, software developers, web designers, and business and creative professionals use Safari Books Online as their primary resource for research, problem solving, learning, and certification training.

Safari Books Online offers a range of plans and pricing for enterprise, government, education, and individuals.

Members have access to thousands of books, training videos, and prepublication manuscripts in one fully searchable database from publishers like O'Reilly Media, Prentice Hall Professional, Addison-Wesley Professional, Microsoft Press, Sams, Que, Peachpit Press, Focal Press, Cisco Press, John Wiley & Sons, Syngress, Morgan Kaufmann, IBM Redbooks, Packt, Adobe Press, FT Press, Apress, Manning, New Riders, McGraw-Hill, Jones & Bartlett, Course Technology, and hundreds more. For more information about Safari Books Online, please visit us online.

How to Contact Us

Please address comments and questions concerning this book to the publisher:

O'Reilly Media, Inc.
1005 Gravenstein Highway North
Sebastopol, CA 95472
800-998-9938 (in the United States or Canada)
707-829-0515 (international or local)
707-829-0104 (fax)

We have a web page for this book, where we list errata, examples, and any additional information. You can access this page at *http://bit.ly/identity-and-data-security*.

To comment or ask technical questions about this book, send email to *bookquestions@oreilly.com*.

For more information about our books, courses, conferences, and news, see our website at *http://www.oreilly.com*.

Find us on Facebook: *http://facebook.com/oreilly*

Follow us on Twitter: *http://twitter.com/oreillymedia*

Watch us on YouTube: *http://www.youtube.com/oreillymedia*

Acknowledgments

First of all we would like to thank the O'Reilly crew for publishing this book and enabling us to share our knowledge, thoughts, and opinions with many individuals around the world. A huge special thanks goes out to our editor, Meg Foley, who has been patient, supportive, and helpful throughout the process of finishing this work.

Our thanks also go out to Lenny Markus, Allen Tom, and Aaron Parecki, who patiently reviewed this book's manuscript and helped to improve its quality tremendously.

We'd also like to thank our developer relations team for proofreading, providing critique, and freeing us up to work on this book.

Finally, we'd like to express our gratitude to you, our readers, for buying this book. We hope you enjoy it!

Jonathan

I'd like to start out by thanking my partner in crime, Tim, for being an amazing co-author to work with. Without our continued conversations, building up and breaking down all of our ideas into new amazing hybrids of their original selves, this book wouldn't be what it is today. Your ideas, drive, and humor made this one of my favorite experiences.

To my wife, Heather, you've helped to keep me sane when I decided to write my first book almost five years ago. Despite the fact that I forgot how much time away that took, you stood by me when I decided to write another one. Without you, I could not have kept my sanity and drive throughout this process. You have always been by my side to encourage me to chase my dreams. You've been my biggest advocate through all of this, and I love you for that.

To my daughter, Scarlett, throughout the time that I have had to pleasure to be your father, you have brought a calming effect into my life. With constant chaos, you have allowed me to see that the world doesn't have to be as serious as I used to think it was. You've brought a peace into my life that I will always thank you for.

To my group, my friends. We may all go our separate ways, be split through companies and across the world, but I will always see you as some of my closest friends. We have been through so much together and have sacrificed a lot. Despite all that, you have been our supporters through everything we have gone through, boosting us up, allowing us to succeed. Thank you.

Tim

I'd like to thank Jonathan, who's not only been a fantastic colleague and friend, but also a great coauthor on this book. It was brilliant to be able to bounce ideas and thoughts back and forth, and I am positive that the book would have been far less interesting without your influence, support, and work.

My wife, Karin, deserves a huge thank you—and probably an even bigger bouquet of flowers—for granting me all the time I needed in order to finish my work on this book.

Joe Nash, Alan Wong, Steven Cooper, and Cristiano Betta have been a fantastic team throughout the time of authoring this book and deserve to be mentioned here.

I am grateful for everyone who encouraged me to write this piece and saw me rambling about security concepts and usability concepts on various stages.

A special mention goes to Danese Cooper, PayPal's Head of Open Source, who strongly encouraged me to write down my thoughts beyond blog posts.

Finally, I would like to thank both John Lunn and Taylor Nguyen, who supported me tremendously in writing this book and gave me support and advice throughout my career.

CHAPTER 1

Introduction

Jonathan LeBlanc and Tim Messerschmidt

One of the most important investments that you can make in a system, company, or application is in your security and identity infrastructures. We can't go a week without hearing about another user/customer data breach, stolen credit cards, or identity theft. Even though you can put an entire series of hurdles in the way of a potential attacker, the possibility will always exist that your databases will be breached, information will be stolen, and an attacker will attempt to crack the sensitive data that is stored (if encrypted).

There is no bulletproof, secure method for protecting your data. Identity and data security has always been about mitigating risk, protecting the secure data, and buying yourself enough time to take action and reduce damage if something like this should ever happen to you.

As we dive down into the concepts, technology, and programming methodologies behind building a secure interface for data and identity, you will explore the trade offs and core concepts that you need to understand as you embark on making those final decisions about your security. The best place to start is to explore the major problems with identity and data security in the industry right now.

The Problems with Current Security Models

The current state of industry security is not one in which the technology can't keep up with the potential attack vectors, it's one in which development choices lead us down a path of weak systems. One of the biggest mistakes that many of us tend to make is to assume that users will understand how to protect their own accounts, such as with strong password choices or two-factor authentication—or even if they do, that they wouldn't pick the most usable choice over the easiest one. We, as developers, have to protect our users in the same way that we try to protect our systems, and we must assume that users will not do that for themselves.

To do that, we have to purge a few misconceptions from our heads:

Users will always use the most secure options
> The simple fact is that the worst thing to count on is that users will be capable, or willing, to use the option that will best secure their data. The onus has to be on the site or service owner to ensure that data provided by users for their security (such as a password) is hardened to ensure that minimum levels of security are imposed (see more about data encryption and security in Chapter 2). For instance, when two-factor authentication services are offered, a typical adoption rate is approximately between 5% and 10% of users.

We should always make systems more secure, at the cost of usability
> This is typically one of the reactions to the preceding point—to make a system as secure as possible, at the cost of usability of the system for the user. This is simply not the case; numerous mechanisms can be put in place to enhance security without drastically affecting the user. We'll explore this further in "Security over Usability" on page 4.

Our security will never be breached
> From startups to large companies, many engineers have put too much faith in the security of their systems. This has led to lax data encryption standards, meaning that personal and privileged information, such as credit card data, home addresses, etc., is stored as cleartext—data that is not encrypted in any way. When the system is breached, hackers have to put in no effort to capture and use that data.

 Assume Your Data Will Be Stolen and Use Proper Data Encryption

In June 2015, a massive breach of US government data was said to expose the personal information of millions of government workers, because the data itself was not encrypted.[1] No matter how big you are, you should always assume that the possibility exists that your database security will be breached, and data stolen. All sensitive information should always be properly encrypted.

Let's drill down into some of these issues a bit further to see the cause and effect of the choices we make as users and developers.

---

[1] Computer World (*http://www.computerworld.com/article/2935132/cybercrime-hacking/hacked-data-on-millions-of-us-govt-workers-was-unencrypted.html*)

Poor Password Choices

As we stated previously, users are notorious for choosing highly unsecure passwords for their accounts. To expand on that proof point, let's look at the top passwords of 2015 (listed in Table 1-1), compiled by SplashData from files containing millions of stolen passwords that have been posted online during the previous year.[2]

Table 1-1. Most popular passwords of 2015

1: 123456	6: 123456/89	11: welcome	16: dragon	21: princess
2: password	7: football	12: 1234567890	17: master	22: qwertyuiop
3: 12345678	8: 1234	13: abc123	18: monkey	23: solo
4: qwerty	9: 1234567	14: 111111	19: letmein	24: passw0rd
5: 12345	10: baseball	15: 1qaz2wsx	20: login	25: starwars

Before we get too far up in arms about people choosing these passwords, we need to be aware of some possible issues with the data used to compile this list:

- Because most of this data comes from information leaks, it could be that these passwords are just easier to crack through dictionary or brute-force attacks.

- We don't know the source of much of this data, so we can't validate the security measures in place on the sites or services.

- The data may contain anomalies or simply bad data. If a default password is being set by a service with a lot of leaked data (and never changed), it will push it higher on the list. If we are analyzing data from multiple sources using information that was poorly parsed, or has those anomalies, the list will be skewed.

With that said, even though those passwords may constitute a smaller number than the lists purport them to be, and the data may be highly skewed, they still exist. When building a data and identity security system, you have to provide an adequate level of protection for these people. Typically, you want to build for the weakest possible authentication system, which, depending on your security requirements, might comprise this list.

In many ways this is because of what we expect of people when they are creating a password: provide a password with mixed case, at least one symbol and number, and nothing recognizable in a dictionary or guessable from those who know you. These types of expectations create poor usability for users, in that they won't be able to remember the password, and also ensures that they either pick the easiest way they

---

2 *http://www.teamsid.com/worst-passwords-2015*

can to enter the site, or write down that complex password on a Post-it note on their display. Usability needs to be a part of identity security for it to be effective.

Security over Usability

> Favor security too much over the experience and you'll make the website a pain to use.
>
> —Anthony T, founder of UX Movement

Your main objective when handling the data and identity of your users is to ensure their security, but at the same time you don't want to alienate your entire user base by making your sign-in forms complex, or by forcing a multiscreen, manual checkout process for purchasing goods, or by continually challenging users for identification details as they are trying to use your service. Those are surefire ways of ensuring that your users never return.

 Some of the main reasons for shopping-cart abandonment include users being uncomfortable with the buying process (it is too complex/lengthy) or being forced to sign-up before purchasing. Many of these concerns can be solved through the usability considerations, such as a single-page checkout, and allowing a simplified guest checkout.

The concept of usability versus security is always a balancing act. You need to ensure that you have a high-enough confidence in the security of your users, and at the same time do as much behind the scenes as you can so that they aren't forced to break out of the experience of your site to continually verify themselves.

Here are some of the questions that we can ask ourselves, when thinking this through, are:

- Can I obtain identity information to increase my confidence that the user is who she says she is, without imposing additional security checks?
- If I have a high confidence that the user is who she says she is, can I build a more usable experience for that user versus one that I have no confidence in?
- What content requires user identification, and when should I impose additional levels of security to verify that?

We'll explore these concepts further in Chapter 3, as you learn about trust zones and establishing identity information on a user.

Improper Data Encryption

Data security and identification isn't about planning for the best, it's about planning for the worst. If there is the possibility of something happening, you should assume that it will happen and have a plan in place to decrease or mitigate the damage that is done.

On March 27, 2015, Slack announced that its systems had been breached, and user information was stolen. The damage of the security incident was lessened because of its strong data encryption methods. From the company's blog on the incident, "Slack maintains a central user database that includes usernames, email addresses, and one-way encrypted (*hashed*) passwords. Slack's hashing function is bcrypt with a randomly generated salt per password, which makes it computationally infeasible that your password could be re-created from the hashed form." In addition, following this incident, Slack introduced two-factor authentication for users, as well as a password kill switch for team owners that automatically logged out all users, on all devices, and forced them to create a new password.

In this case, data encryption and quick action prevented a massive theft of user accounts, and lessened the damage to Slack's credibility and the confidence its users had in the company. Data encryption isn't always about trying to prevent data from being stolen; it's meant to slow down hackers long enough to make it infeasible for them to decrypt massive amounts of data, or to delay them until you can take appropriate action.

The Weakest Link: Human Beings

As developers and service providers, our biggest interest should be treating our users' data with the most respect we can provide. Hence, we try to secure any kind of information a user provides to us by using encryption algorithms, offer safe ways to communicate, and continuously harden our infrastructure in an ongoing struggle.

The most important element in this chain, the human being, is often taken out of the equation. Therefore, we open up our application to threats that we might not have considered when laying out and designing our security layer. The truth is, users tend to go the easy way. People are likely to choose easy-to-remember and short passwords, simple-to-guess usernames, and might not be educated about current authentication technology like two-factor authentication (also known as 2FA). We discuss two-factor authentication in depth in Chapter 5—it certainly deserves extra attention and focus. We will also discuss a technology derived from 2FA, called n-factor authentication, which represents a scalable security approach depending on the use case.

It is easy to understand why people tend to use and especially reuse simple passwords —it saves them time while setting up user profiles and makes authenticating against services and applications an easy task. Especially with the rise of mobile technology, users are often faced with small screen real estate and touchscreen keyboards, which can add an additional burden.

The phenomenon described here is also known as *password fatigue*. Gladly, there are multiple tools that we, as developers, can use in order to counter these problems and ensure a smooth and pleasing registration and authentication flow within our applications while still maintaining user security.

 Many operating systems, browsers, and third-party applications try to solve password fatigue by allowing users to generate randomized passwords and by offering a way to store those passwords under protection of a master password.

A popular example is the password-management application Keychain that was introduced with Mac OS 8.6. Keychain is deeply integrated into OS X and nowadays in iOS (via iCloud) and allows for storing various types of data including credit cards, passwords, and private keys.

More and more services like 1Password, Dashlane, and LastPass offer to generate passwords for their users. This removes the need for users to come up with a secure password and is often seen as a convenient way to speed up user account registration.

Katie Sherwin, a member of the Nielsen Norman Group, proposes simplifying password authentication flows through three approaches that improve user experience:[3]

- Show the rules
- Show the user input
- Show strength meters

By applying these three rules, we can ensure that users feel comfortable with the passwords they use and get a clear indication about the password's strength. Further research indicates that users who see a strength meter choose more secure passwords —even if the strength indicator is not implemented that well.[4]

> Those who saw a meter tended to choose stronger passwords than those who didn't, but the type of meter did not make a significant difference.
>
> —Dinei Florencio, Cormac Herley, and Paul C. van Oorschot,
> "An Administrator's Guide to Internet Password Research"

Single Sign-on

Single sign-on, also known as *SSO*, is a technology that leverages existing user accounts in order to authenticate against various services. The idea behind this con-

---

3 *http://www.nngroup.com/articles/password-creation*

4 *http://research.microsoft.com/pubs/227130/WhatsaSysadminToDo.pdf*

cept is prefilling and securing a central user account instead of forcing the user to register at a variety of services over and over again.

Common choices that try to accommodate the wish to reuse user profiles to either provide profile information or to simply authenticate against other services include OpenID, OAuth 1.0, OAuth 2.0, and various hybrid models like OpenID Connect. In Chapter 4 we will focus on a selection of authentication techniques and will discuss the technical implementation details as well as the security implications.

Understanding Entropy in Password Security

Before we get too far into the weeds, we should first address how we can determine a weak password from a strong one, if that password was created by a human being. The standard industry mechanism for determining password strength is called *information entropy*, which is measured in the number of bits of information in a provided source, such as a password.

 Typically, if you are using passphrases, a good level of entropy to have at minimum is 36.86 bits, which coincides with the average entropy level of 3 random words selected from a list of 5,000 possible unique words.

Password entropy is a measurement of how unpredictable a password is. This measurement is based on a few key characteristics:

- The symbol set that is used
- The expansion of the symbol set through lowercase/uppercase characters
- Password length

Using this information, password entropy, expressed in bits, is used to predict how difficult it would be for the password to be cracked through guessing, dictionary attacks, brute-force attacks, etc.

When you are looking at determining overall password entropy, there are two main ways of generating passwords that we should explore: randomly generated passwords (computer generated) and human-selected passwords.

According to "A Large-Scale Study of Web Password Habits," by Dinei Florencio and Cormac Herley of Microsoft Research, the entropy level of the average password is estimated to be 40.54 bits.[5]

Entropy in Randomly Selected Passwords

When we look at randomly selected passwords (computer generated), the process for determining the overall entropy of the passwords is fairly straightforward because there is no human, random element involved. Depending on the symbol set that we use, we can build a series of passwords with a desired level of entropy fairly easily.

First, the generally accepted formula that we use to calculate entropy is $H = log_2(b^l)$

where

- H = The password entropy, measured in bits
- b = The number of possible symbols in the symbol set
- l = The number of symbols in the password (or length)

To come up with the value of b, we can simply choose the symbol set that we are using from Table 1-2.

Table 1-2. Entropy for each symbol in a symbol set

Symbol set name	Number of symbols in set	Entropy per symbol (in bits)
Arabic numerals (0–9)	10	3.322
Hexadecimal numerals (0–9, A–F)	16	4.000
Case-insensitive Latin alphabet (a–z or A–Z)	26	4.700
Case-insensitive alphanumeric (a–z or A-Z, 0–9)	36	5.170
Case-sensitive Latin alphabet (a–z, A–Z)	52	5.700
Case-sensitive alphanumeric (a–z, A–Z, 0–9)	62	5.954
All ASCII printable characters	95	6.570
All extended ASCII printable characters	218	7.768
Binary (0–255 or 8 bits or 1 byte)	256	8.000
Diceware word list	7776	12.925

5 *http://research.microsoft.com/pubs/74164/www2007.pdf*

The symbol set you might not be familiar with is the diceware word list. The method behind diceware is to use a single die (from a pair of dice), and roll it five times. The numeric values on the die each time create a five-digit number (e.g., 46231, matching the value of each individual roll). This number is then used to look up a word from a given word list. There are 7,776 possible unique words using this method. See the diceware word list (*http://world.std.com/ ~reinhold/diceware.wordlist.asc*) for the complete reference.

Using the formula, length of the password, and numbers of symbols in a given symbol set, you can estimate the bits of entropy from a randomly generated password.

Entropy in Human-Selected Passwords

Before we get into measuring entropy levels within a password that was created by a human being, rather than being randomly generated based on security standards, we need to understand that these numbers are nontrivial. Many methods have been proposed for doing so (NIST, Shannon Entropy, Guessing Entropy, etc.), but most of these fall short in one way or another.

Shannon Entropy is seen to give an overly optimistic view of password security (while providing no real actionable improvement hints), and NIST a nonaccurate (yet conservative) one. Because we always want to err on the side of caution with password security, let's quickly look at the NIST study on how to measure human-selected passwords, as that will give us a good starting point.

According to NIST special publication 800-63-2, if we take a human-selected password, we can measure the assumed entropy with the following guidelines:[6]

- The entropy of the first character is 4 bits.
- The entropy of the next 7 characters is 2 bits per character (they state that this is "roughly consistent with Shannon's estimate that *when statistical effects extending over not more than 8 letters are considered, the entropy is roughly 2.3 bits per character*").
- Characters 9 through 20 have an entropy of 1.5 bits per character.
- Characters 21 and above have an entropy of 1 bit per character.
- A 6-bit bonus is given to password rules that *require* both uppercase and nonalphabetic characters. (This is also a conservative bit estimate, as the NIST publication notes that these special characters will most likely come at the beginning or end of the password, reducing the total search space.)

---

6 *http://nvlpubs.nist.gov/nistpubs/SpecialPublications/NIST.SP.800-63-2.pdf*

- An additional 6-bit bonus is given to passwords with a length of 1 to 19 characters that follow an extensive dictionary check to ensure the password is not contained within a large dictionary. Passwords that are longer than 20 characters do not receive this bonus because they are assumed to consist of multiple dictionary words placed together into passphrases.

Let's take that idea and see what the entropy of a few examples would be:

monkey (6 characters) = 14 bits of entropy
    4 bits for the first character, 10 bits for the following 5 characters

Monkey1 (7 characters) = 22 bits of entropy
    4 bits for the first character, 12 bits for the following 6 characters, 6-bit bonus for uppercase and nonalphabetic characters being used

tvMD128!Rrsa (12 characters) = 36 bits of entropy
    4 bits for the first character, 14 bits for the following 7 characters, 6 bits for the following 4 characters, 6-bit bonus for uppercase and nonalphabetic characters being used, 6-bit bonus for a nondictionary string within 1–19 characters

tvMD128!aihdfo#Jh43 (19 characters) = 46.5 bits of entropy
    4 bits for the first character, 14 bits for the following 7 characters, 16.5 bits for the following 11 characters, 6-bit bonus for uppercase and nonalphabetic characters being used, 6-bit bonus for a nondictionary string within 1–19 characters

tvMD128!aihdfo#Jh432 (20 characters) = 42 bits of entropy
    4 bits for the first character, 14 bits for the following 7 characters, 18 bits for the following 12 characters, 6-bit bonus for uppercase and nonalphabetic characters being used

You can start to see some holes in the assumptions that the NIST study makes with the last two password examples. First, one additional character causes the loss of 6 bonus bits of entropy because of the assumption that the password is of significant length that a user would not have chosen a complex string. Second, that if a string of that length was used for a password, it is most likely several dictionary words put together, such as "treemanicuredonkeytornado," which, based on the NIST study, would actually give us 41 bits of entropy.

As we go further, you can see why determining the security of a human-created password can be tricky, and that's because humans are unpredictable. If we plug a system of security requirements into a computer-generated password system, and store that in a password vault application like 1Password, KeePass, or LastPass, then we can have a very predictable environment. That's why, for the most part, we usually take one of two steps (sometimes both) in securing identity in web development:

1. You require users, when they create their password, to strengthen their login. This can be requirements for length, nonalphabetic characters, uppercase and lowercase characters, nondictionary words, etc. For obvious reasons, the usability of this solution is quite bad, and it may alienate many users, but the security increases. The problem here is that when we make it harder to create a password, the user will more likely forget that password, and then require the use of the "forgot your password" reset flow.

2. You attempt to harden the data, as best you can, behind the scenes. This usually involves encryption, salting, and key stretching (all concepts we will dive into in Chapter 2), to try to help prevent weak passwords that are stolen from being compromised. When you have a solution like this, you may also see a mechanism that allows only a certain number of login attempts before temporarily locking the account, to prevent potential brute-force attacks against weak passwords. This solution is higher on the usability side, because users can pick practically any password they want, but lowers the overall security of their account.

In the end, we're back to questions of usability versus security, and the truth of the matter is that our ideal scenario, for all parties, is somewhere in between. Remember, the two aren't mutually exclusive.

Breaking Down System Usage of a Username and Password

Another important step in understanding the concept of a username and password is to break down what they represent in an identification system. If we put this simply, they are an identification of who you are (the username, or public key) and then a verification of that fact with something that only you should know (the password, or private key).

With that understanding in place, there are two ways that we can think about handling data in an authentication system:

Harden the system
> In this case, we take an existing (or new) system that is built on top of a traditional username and password, and attempt to strengthen it.

Remove the username and password
> In new or innovative technology solutions, this is the case where we apply the concepts of a username and password, but do so in a different way.

As we dive further into each chapter, our main goals will be to build upon these two concepts, focusing on hardening the system, or finding a new methodology for building our identity and data security with new tools and techniques.

Securing Our Current Standards for Identity

Enhancing the security of an existing system is usually the choice of most of us, as we are building on top of existing work, or building a product that uses a username and password as the preferred login mechanism for users.

As we explored earlier in this chapter, users are usually the worst people to put in charge of protecting their own security through their passwords. The vast majority of the population will choose passwords that they can remember, which is almost always the complete opposite of what we would traditionally think of as a secure password.

You know from earlier sections how to approximate the predictability of a password, and that you should always build security toward the most unsecure element in the chain, not the average. With that said, there are certain standard mechanisms that we use for account security, and others that we should avoid.

Good and Bad Security Algorithms

Not all encryption algorithms are created equal when it comes to the security of our data and privileged user information. Some are built for speed, for quickly and accurately encrypting and decrypting large amounts of data. Others are designed to be slow. Let's say your database of a million encrypted user records has been stolen, and the attacker is attempting to crack the encryption, such as by trying every word in the dictionary, to reveal the data underneath. Would you prefer to make this as fast as possible or as slow as possible? The correct answer is that you want this process to be as slow as possible for the attacker.

With regular cryptographic hash functions, an attacker can guess billions of passwords per second. With password security hashing algorithms, depending on the configuration, the attacker may be able to guess only a few thousand passwords per second, which is a massive difference.

The good

The following hashing algorithms are meant to be used for password security, and are built to be purposefully slow to make cracking the data harder:

PBKDF2
> PBKDF2 stands for *Password-Based Key Derivation Function 2*, and was created by RSA Laboratories. It applies a pseudorandom function, such as a hash, cipher, or HMAC, to the input (password) along with a salt. The process is repeated many times, which produces a derived key.

bcrypt
> Created by Niels Provos and David Mazières, bcrypt stands for *Belgian Fundamental Research in Cryptology and Information Security*. It is a key derivation

function based on the blowfish cipher. It incorporates a salt into the process to protect the key, and also has an interesting adaptive functionality to it. Over time, the iteration count can be increased to make it slower, so it remains resistant to brute-force attacks.

scrypt
> Created by Colin Percival, scrypt is another key derivation function that is designed to combat large-scale hardware attacks by requiring high amounts of memory and therefore slowing down computation.

The bad (for passwords)

The following are our standard cryptographic hashing algorithms, which are meant to be fast. In the case of password security, this is not a good scenario because slowing down the algorithm makes it much harder for an attacker to crack the data:

MD5
> MD5, or *message-digest algorithm*, was designed by Robert Rivest in 1991, and produces a 128-bit hash value, typically expressed as a 32-digit hexadecimal number.

SHA-1
> SHA stands for *Secure Hash Algorithm*. Designed by the NSA, SHA-1 produces a 160-bit (20-byte) hash value. This hash value is typically rendered as a 40-digit hexadecimal number.

SHA-2
> Also designed by the NSA, SHA-2 is the successor of SHA-1, and consists of six hash functions with hash values that are 224, 256, 384, or 512 bits (SHA-224, SHA-256, SHA-384, SHA-512, SHA-512/224, SHA-512/256).

What Data Should Be Protected?

We've hinted at this a few times during this chapter, but when it comes to asking yourself, "What information absolutely needs to be encrypted?" the answer is pretty simple: anything that is personally identifiable (identity data, personal information, payment details), or anything that is imperative to your system that could open up additional leaks or holes in your architecture if released.

Account Recovery Mechanisms and Social Engineering

After we've reviewed the details worth protecting, we should take this knowledge into account when looking at recovery mechanisms. Often social engineering or weak recovery mechanisms lead to exposure of information—even though protection mechanisms were implemented in order to prevent exactly this. If you are familiar with these matters, feel free to skip to this chapter's wrap-up.

Popular examples include customer support providing account details they're not supposed to share, and badly planned password-reset flows. A compromised email account can lead to easy access to a user's account—securing our users by offering sensible security questions and allowing them to provide specific responses can help lower the risk of information leaks.

> Social engineering is a non-technical method of intrusion hackers use that relies heavily on human interaction and often involves tricking people into breaking normal security procedures. It is one of the greatest threats that organizations today encounter.[7]
>
> —TechTarget SearchSecurity

The Problem with Security Questions

While the overall knowledge and consciousness about secure passwords is steadily growing, another volatile area—security questions—is often ignored. Instead of offering users an array of personal questions or even allowing for the definition of their own security questions, many generic phrases are offered that are often as easy to find out as searching for a person's social media profile.

Security questions often appear as repetitive and sometimes even inadvertently comedic collections that can be cumbersome to answer and hard to remember ("What was my favorite dish as a child?" "What's your favorite book?"). Soheil Rezayazdi published a list of Nihilistic Security Questions on McSweeney's Internet Tendency that should at least cause a slight smile on your face—here are our personal top five:[8]

1. When did you stop trying?
2. In what year did you abandon your dreams?
3. At what age did your childhood pet run away?
4. What was the name of your favorite unpaid internship?
5. What is the name of your least favorite child?

In all seriousness, the impact of social engineering is often completely underestimated or even ignored. It is often easier to pass barriers instead of circumventing and breaking them down. The scope of social engineering can be anything between looking up some facts about a person online and sneaking into office buildings; while this

---

7 *http://searchsecurity.techtarget.com/definition/social-engineering*

8 *http://www.mcsweeneys.net/articles/nihilistic-password-security-questions*

might sound like an exaggeration (and often does not have to happen), it makes sense to prepare and train staff accordingly.

If you are looking for more information on this topic, great resources on social engineering are Kevin Mitnick's books *Ghost in the Wires* (Back Bay Books), *The Art of Intrusion* (Wiley), and *The Art of Deception* (Wiley).[9]

Next Up

Now that you understand all of the concepts that we are going to be using and talking about throughout the rest of the chapters, let's jump into the next chapter by drilling down into how hashing, salting, and data encryption can be added to your systems.

---

9 Kevin Mitnick rose to mainstream fame by hacking companies such as Nokia and Pacific Bell. He's currently active as a security consultant.

CHAPTER 2

Password Encryption, Hashing, and Salting

Jonathan LeBlanc

In the first chapter you learned about the underlying concepts of password security, and the current state of the industry and standards that are employed. Let's start putting some of that into practice as we explore the practical application of password encryption and security. To start this implementer's approach, let's first look at the ways that data can be transmitted and stored.

Data at Rest Versus Data in Motion

As we start to explore the concepts of data security, there are two important concepts that we should address: data in motion versus data at rest.

When we talk about *data at rest*, we mean the inactive (or resting) digital data that is being stored on your servers, such as the databases that you are using to store passwords, profile information, or any other details needed within your application.

When we discuss the concept of *data in motion*, we're talking about any data that is in transit, being sent back and forth from an application to a database, or communication back and forth between websites and APIs or external data sources.

Data at Rest

> If you're talking about credit card environments, where you've got a requirement to encrypt the credit card information at rest, I think the most common method people use there is enabling encryption within the database. That's typically about as good as it gets in terms of host-based encryption.[1]
>
> —Chris Gatford, Hacklabs

Web and application developers rarely have to encounter the concept of protecting the database that stores secure information about our clients, but it is a concept that should be understood. While the technical aspects of data at rest are beyond the scope of this book, let's cover some of the basic concepts and guidelines to understand that database encryption is absolutely needed, even though in 99% of organizations, this is simply not done.

As we've tried to reiterate on a few occassions, you should always assume a worst-case scenario when planning for data breaches. In this case, we should assume that an attacker has gained access to our database, with the end goal of capturing any sensitive data and passwords. Wouldn't you want to have both the password encryption to prevent account access, as well as an additional layer of encryption on the database itself?

First, let's address the encryption methods that should be used on the database. Different from the standards that we discussed in Chapter 1 for password encryption, the strong encryption methods that should be used for database encryption are SHA-256 (Secure Hash Algorithm) or better, AES (Advanced Encryption Standard), and RSA (Rivest-Shamir-Adleman). These are all part of the NIST-approved algorithms.[2] Weak encryption algorithms, such as MD5 and SHA-1, should never be used for database encryption.

Now, a few standards should be followed:

- Keep access control (user login) separate from database encryption. Should a username or password fail, the database itself should remain encrypted, effectively providing multiple levels of protection.
- The keys used for database encryption should be updated on a regular basis.
- Encryption keys should always be stored separately from the data.

Data federation is another method to help prevent unwanted access in the case of an application with global reach and data storage. The purpose of this strategy is to

---

1 *http://www.zdnet.com/article/encrypting-data-at-rest-is-vital-but-its-just-not-happening*

2 *http://csrc.nist.gov/publications/nistpubs/800-57/sp800-57_part1_rev3_general.pdf*

maintain distinct database systems in the regions where the personal information is needed (e.g., the personal information of a UK customer is stored within a database in the UK, not a centralized database in the US). Effectively, instead of having a centralized database with all customer information that is copied around to data centers as needed, only information in the region in which it is needed is maintained. This type of strategy is effective when government regulations/laws require access to be granted to all user information that is stored in their country, regardless of whether that data belongs to individuals in other countries.

Lastly, one underlying concept should be understood and implemented. You should store only the minimum amount of sensitive user data that is required to run your application, site, or services. A major industry trend over the past few years has been to capture as much information about your users as possible, store it, and then figure out whether it is useful and is viable at a later date. This is *absolutely not* the practice that should be employed when you are trying to provide the best level of protection for your users. When creating the architectural schema for your application or website, you should consider the type of data that is needed for the state of the application, and use that to build the database structure for personal information that should be stored. The less privileged information you store, the less potential impact on your customers.

Beyond the user data, sensitive financial information such as credit card data can also be offloaded, typically to the payment provider through a system such as a credit card vault. In addition to the security benefits of not having to host that data yourself, you don't incur the implications of having to implement all standards for PCI DSS compliance, as required when hosting payment information for customers.[3]

Data in Motion

Data in motion, or data that is in transit, is what the vast majority of web and application developers will be dealing with in their day-to-day work. Realistically, this will encompass several scenarios, including these:

- Signup information from a user that will be used for account access and identity
- Transmission of profile information to and from service APIs
- Other data collected through the application or website and transmitted for database storage

This is the data focus that we will be exploring throughout the upcoming chapters. Our first step is to look into security and encryption behind the user profile, through the proper storage and use of the user password.

---

3 *https://www.pcisecuritystandards.org/security_standards*

Password Attack Vectors

There are many ways for an attacker to attempt to gain access to user accounts. Some are geared toward manipulation of the users themselves, while others attempt to target the application or website to gain access. A few of these are as follows:

Phishing

Tricking users into providing their login credentials through a malicious site or application. Typically, you see these types of attempts come through email scams, where the sender pretends to be the company in question, and requires users to log in to the malicious site for some reason, thereby stealing their login credentials and access to their accounts.

Social engineering

Taking the concept behind phishing to a new level, social engineering hacks are usually orchestrated by other communication means, such as through phone calls. The attacker pretends to be a network technician, or some sort of IT security for a company, and asks users for their login credentials to repair the issue that they are calling about. In doing so, they gain access to the user account.

As you can well imagine, it is difficult to build a safety net for cases such as these, but when it comes to attacks against the website or application that we are working with, we definitely can build safety measures into our login controls, profile systems, and database structures. These attack vectors include the following:

Brute-force attacks

Calculating every possible key variation within a given length, and then trying each one, one after another, until the password is guessed. The shorter the password, the faster this method works. As the length of the password increases, the time to crack the password increases exponentially. When this method becomes too costly, other methods, such as dictionary attacks, are employed. One of the methods employed to counter brute-force attacks is key stretching, which we'll explore later in this chapter.

Dictionary attacks

Looping through a list of predetermined words/terms, such as all words in a dictionary (hence the term *dictionary attack*), and trying all combinations against an encrypted password to find matching values. Unlike a brute-force attack, a dictionary attack is just trying input that is considered to, most likely, be a common input word, term, or phrase. Use of a salt (which we'll discuss in "Salting" on page 32) is an appropriate way of dealing with these types of attacks.

Rainbow tables
> Large lists that contain precalculated hashes (for a given hash function), and the passwords from which they were derived. Unlike a dictionary attack, where the hash function is applied at each crack attempt, the attacker can simply compare the precalculated hash with the password hash from the user database, making the entire process more efficient. Use of a salt is an appropriate way of dealing with these types of attacks. This type of attack is typically carried out offline, when the attacker has full access to the data.

Malware
> Key loggers or screen scrapers that might be present on a user's machine, logging activity during login or sign-up. Typically, these are used in conjunction with social engineering to prompt the user to load or install a piece of infected content. An appropriate way of dealing with these attacks is to use a second factor of authentication (e.g., text-message verification) during login.

Offline cracking
> We cannot forget that there's always the possibility that all of our stored user information will be stolen, giving attackers all the time they want to crack a password hash. Once the data is stolen, hardening techniques such as hashing our passwords with a salt, and using appropriate hashing mechanisms that are built to slow down cracking, are the barriers to data theft.

With an understanding of the general landscape of attack vectors, let's dig into some of these in more depth.

Brute-Force Attack

Brute-force attacks, also known as an *exhaustive key search*, is the practice of attempting to break password encryption by going through all potential permutations of a password for a given length. In trying to break a password of a known length, up to five characters, a brute-force attack will attempt every possible password permutation of that length.

Obviously, this is not the first method that an attacker would use, because of the length of time that it would take to crack a password. For a password with a key length of N *bits*, the time that it would take to crack the password would be proportional to the number of bits, which would be proportional to 2^N in the worst case, but half of that on average. Thus, as the password length increases, the time to break the password also increases, exponentially.

Other methods, such as the use of rainbow tables or dictionary attacks, are more viable attack vectors. Typically, brute-force attacks will be used with only offline data (not a direct site attack, but data that was downloaded in a hack), and will be used only when other more viable vectors are unavailable to the attacker. If proper password encryption methods are employed that utilize key stretching, this attack method becomes incredibly negligable.

Given these facts, when it does come to securing your web application from potential brute-force attacks, various methods can be implemented to prevent this attack vector:

- Implementing a CAPTCHA (Completely Automated Public Turing test to tell Computers and Humans Apart) following an unsuccessful login attempt to increase login complexity and help prevent automated attacks.
- Adding in a 2FA (two-factor authentication) verification mechanism, such as through an SMS to a verified phone number using Authy (*https://www.authy.com*) or a similar service.

We'll go through an implementation of 2FA with Authy in Chapter 5, but let's see what a CAPTCHA implementation might look like when integrated within our site.

Creating a CAPTCHA with reCAPTCHA

One of the methods that we can employ for preventing an attacker from attempting password after password is to use a CAPTCHA. Typically, you'll want to use a CAPTCHA only after one to two failed password attempts. It could be that a user has simply forgotten his password, or an attacker could be trying different password combinations in an attempted brute-force attack.

Using a CAPTCHA

As with most security precautions, you want to try to impact users as little as possible. We don't want to show a CAPTCHA for every login attempt, because it's just an extra step that a user has to go through to log in. When restricting use after only one to two failed attempts, you ensure that the vast majority of your users are not impacted, and those who are will mostly understand the reasons for the added security on successive password attempts.

One of the leading CAPTCHA systems is reCAPTCHA by Google (*https://www.google.com/recaptcha/intro/index.html*). It provides a very nice and simple user interface that typically just asks users to click a box to confirm they are not a robot. Your users aren't heavily impacted as with traditional CAPTCHA systems that require you to type in words from a picture or audio recording, and it still provides high levels of security against potential bots and automated attacks.

With that said, let's see how we're going to implement reCAPTCHA on one of our sites, and then confirm user input on our Node server. The first step is to head over to the reCAPTCHA admin page (*https://www.google.com/recaptcha/admin*) to sign-up for an API key pair for our site that will allow us to use the system. On this page (given that we don't have any existing keys), we are met with the registration system that looks like Figure 2-1.

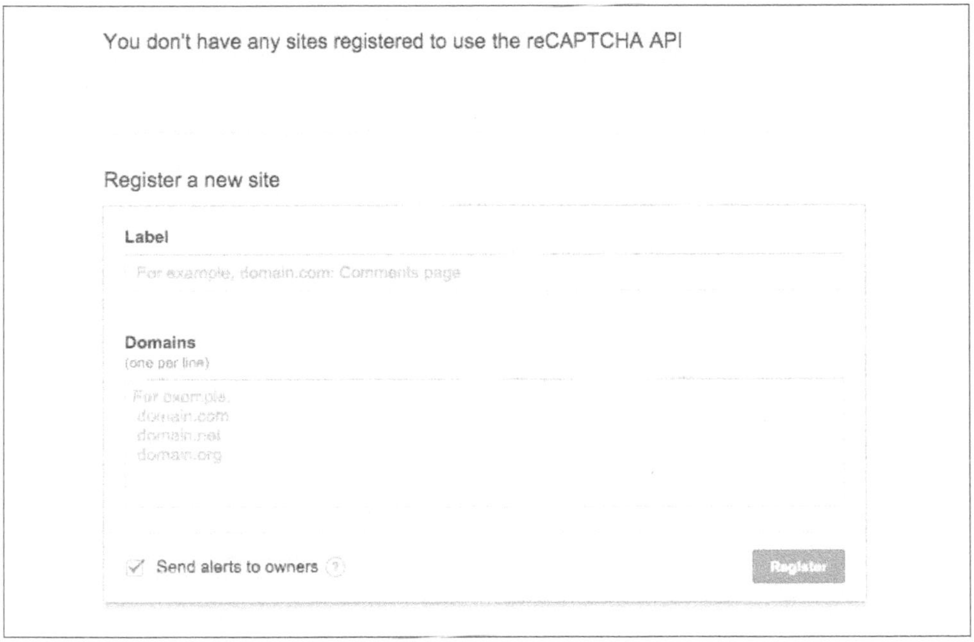

You don't have any sites registered to use the reCAPTCHA API

Register a new site

Label

For example, domain.com: Comments page

Domains
(one per line)

For example,
domain.com
domain.net
domain.org

✓ Send alerts to owners ⑦   Register

Figure 2-1. Registering our keys

Following the instructions on the page to register a new site, we enter a few pieces of information:

Label
Something to identify the site or keys for ourself, such as the site name or URL.

Domains
The root domains that we will be placing reCAPTCHA on. This can be multiple domains that we maintain.

When we click the Register button, we now see all of the setup information that we need to go through to integrate reCAPTCHA on our site, as shown in Figure 2-2.

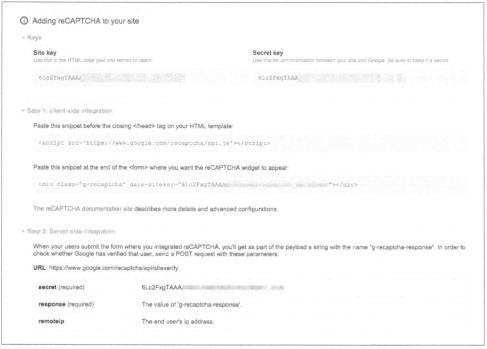

Figure 2-2. Adding reCAPTCHA to our site

At the top we can see the keys that we will be using for this process. Keep those in mind as we go through the two steps that are needed for integration.

First we need to add the reCAPTCHA script include at the end of the <head> section of our HTML document, and create the container for the widget within our login form. Stripping down this process into just the pieces that we need on the page, the HTML code looks like this:

```
<html>
<head>
    <script src='https://www.google.com/recaptcha/api.js'></script>
</head>
<body>

<form method="post" action="/capture">
    <div class="g-recaptcha" data-sitekey="6Lc2FxgTAAAXXXXXXXXXXXXXX"></div>
    <input type="submit" value="Submit">
</form>

</body>
</html>
```

Let's walk through the code to see what we're doing:

- We add the *https://www.google.com/recaptcha/api.js* script include right before the closing </head> tag of our HTML document.

- We create a form that will POST the login data to our Node endpoint, /capture (we will set up an Express app to capture POST requests to that endpoint).

- In the form, we simply have the <div> that will house the reCAPTCHA widget (placed where we want it to show up in the form), and a Submit button to submit the form to our server side endpoint.

When we load that form, we should see something like Figure 2-3, clearly showing the reCAPTCHA widget, with our Submit button below that.

Figure 2-3. reCAPTCHA on our site

The user will interact with the widget and click (or not) the option to identify themselves as human. When the form is submitted, the POST data will be sent to our /capture endpoint. For the reCAPTCHA component, the data we will need to capture for the verification step will be located within the g-recaptcha-response parameter, and look something like this:

```
g-recaptcha-response=03AHJ_VusWHPddH611975sAE4rH9twXhs05HZcIlUa4Yv9eczU_aFxLl2VeB
kisEkZdCBd7a1R35rNvCikbsgkAsEN8KoP400SEFhzNebZN3yaK4826QQT2W0jjaK-fGIVxWGiTzHrcBW
roHDAbImEpukdJj58yN_vJFsgrnSvmXV3jWK09f_zqiOpOw07V848yYnXnIQdCuqR3SKJEvexIEmlRewZ
GnJvnN2pKMaQ_Hcnjp5p2mc5Nm-z_bELGwf2isrQvw8zm9m4lA9Ftu0CS-N3PwZ_R0kELWdSTwNYH7aI8
wlWMHct8A71LDy_t82maP0jC07y6sVzlRJLQ5dsJ5gXCpnuUDPTfeASoJosTUChPPXjYWDEiZ8dAJxxNP
SNdyhftEXtrN7PiebkIEVngwRxVUqZRLe9JQpLk9HimOoOuuu5gKva4Ai_-ohHHqaAem6e_AJe6GnWO8f
PDpqXBcNOU_kkDOfQ_zHZ7FVoOvhbBW8GwV5xRjOB-7yxibHguemcm2X22W2atX0TC_hIaJZjWYZncGms
3Hqeq5lITKzInV1W6klHmCvGqCVi akllHjUn1ttQppXsPZyWPx6RWzNKR0Mloe8bYefx2VdYZAhXeJfDMSD
sq1c7KYGJctNXiL34QIGwWxyPkUCYUxMHACkGyryRCxbYKDwi6fdsONeQHe4nhGwFneKU4kI4Kp ymEgc
HvDUaTGS8sLrXiY36eKZrB6CIS0P4pQbJr4TJvt2dE9VkVPjKsyvRKMONpIu6G0pJsxb0ssUHHa_iTK7w
s0k681LM7LKH_MxtQJKwl8_6HycyhDn-BAjx8YEZ-KSslUvuVSelSxEo1R_y_n5MGo-qrRVSmKjP14O2k
DBF0vlW1UZTIgl2gc6Iz_QU6Oz6JQOUJOAZNtkMv6aWu5h-uVkMcIRqIHWWFqg
```

At this point, we need to set up that /capture endpoint to accept the form POST from our HTML document. We'll be using Express for this one, with mostly standard packages. Because we will be dealing with JSON responses, the only package that we'll need to pull down from NPM is body-parser, to handle those responses. We start out by installing this via the following terminal command:

```
npm install body-parser --save
```

Next, let's set up the variables for the packages that we'll need, as well as the configuration for body-parser to handle JSON data responses:

```
var querystring = require('querystring'),
    bodyParser = require('body-parser'),
    https = require('https'),
    app = require('express')();

//support JSON & URL encoded bodies
app.use(bodyParser.json());
app.use(bodyParser.urlencoded({
    extended: true
}));
```

Here is what each package will be used for:

querystring
Converting JSON objects into strings for POSTing

body-parser
Accepting JSON responses from the verification step

https
Making HTTPS requests to verify the reCAPTCHA data sent from the previous form

app
Express

Now let's build an app handler for the data that will be POSTed from our previous form to the /capture endpoint. That block looks like this:

```
//handle all POST requests
app.post('/capture', function (req, res){
    var response = req.body['g-recaptcha-response'];

    var verify_data = querystring.stringify({
        'secret' : 'YOUR SECRET KEY',
        'response': response
    });

    //uber access token fetch endpoint
    var verify_options = {
        host: 'google.com',
        path: '/recaptcha/api/siteverify',
        method: 'POST',
        headers: {
            'Content-Type': 'application/x-www-form-urlencoded',
            'Content-Length': verify_data.length
        }
    };
```

```
//set up request
var post_req = https.request(verify_options, function(result){
    result.setEncoding('utf8');
    result.on('data', function (verification){
        console.log(verification);
    });
});

//post data
post_req.write(verify_data);
post_req.end();
});
```

This code will run for all POSTed data sent to the /capture endpoint. When data arrives, we run it through several steps:

1. We capture the reCAPTCHA data to be verified within the POSTed data, located within req.body[g-recaptcha-response].

2. We build the POST object that will be needed to send to the verification endpoint. The data required will be our secret (this is the key that was given to us at the beginning of this section when we signed up for our keys) and the response from the POST body.

3. We then build out the endpoint data for the verification step. The endpoint to send this data is *https://www.google.com/recaptcha/api/siteverify*, so we set the host to *google.com*, the path to */recaptcha/api/siteverify*, and the method should be POST.

4. We set up the request. Because this is an HTTPS endpoint, we need to use https.request(…), passing along the endpoint option variable that we just created. When the results from that come back, we will simply be logging out the response.

5. We begin the request by sending through the verification data variable that we set up at the beginning.

The last line is to start our server:

```
app.listen(process.env.PORT || 3000);
```

If we run this on localhost, it will listen on port 3000.

At this point, the verification has been sent, and a response on whether this is a human or not (that the person clicked the "I'm not a robot" box) will be logged out from our code.

If successful, the data response that we will see will look like this:

```
{
  "success": true
}
```

If not successful, we'll see a response like this:

```
{
  "success": false,
  "error-codes": [
    "missing-input-response"
  ]
}
```

Basically, if we read the success parameter from the response, we can see whether we should process the login.

Using this method, we can prevent an automated script from simply making request after request to our login for a given username, passing through every possible variation of a password that it can generate, leading to an account being compromised.

Dictionary Attacks

A *dictionary attack* is slightly different from a brute-force attack. Instead of trying every permutation of a given password length, a dictionary attack takes words from a pre-arranged list (typically all words in a dictionary and other common password choices), encrypts those words, and compares the encrypted string against the encrypted password obtained from a user's account.

In a practical sense, let's say that we had each of the words that we wanted to check, such as the following (as just an example):

```
var words = ['animal', 'monkey', 'test', 'tornado', 'mango', 'slide', 'pepper',
             'diaper', 'tube', 'cloth', 'hair', 'smell', 'eyes', 'tip', 'right',
             'wrong', 'happy'];
```

Now, to conduct this type of attack, we would encrypt those words, perhaps with an obtained salt (a random unique string used to strengthen weak passwords) from a data breach, or perhaps without a salt, to give us a hash to compare. Given the words, we might now have the list of hashes shown in Table 2-1.

From our data dump, let's say the user record has an encrypted password of $2a$10$TFKgAYZrfb7p/J6Mz1NZsuhlp62Sa24GKBb7G8q4j7O2rc1Ntlopa. We compare all of the hashes that we have produced against that user hash, and find a match with the word *mango*. We now have a cracked password that we can use to gain access to the user account.

Table 2-1. Dictionary words and associated hashes

Common word	Associated hash
test	$2a$10$wkmirMIMsQxpSvKpn.KNyOTU65YuneDcMXwA7XEHR5brjhpjugWCm
animal	$2a$10$.hfSmZVMv3kv5SE9hMun8O5p/AAWsH7eOrhfYdItG0UCaU/aRT85W
tornado	$2a$10$GI5itVWvmom3vBLTCSsZJ.vUtp5qzAnjVUK5PG4PRIblelkw8BldC
monkey	$2a$10$mmKLHtnYIlvGrcwF9pXgjOEkczGm99f/iNU3qCA2G0ySPgOjAeguO
pepper	$2a$10$wbNHHKyHhIhToY6kpExOZO.qIS4UURMm7sKAUTLudiiyMO8wD.HGq
slide	$2a$10$/j9vzCZqmGvhGLMUFhwJ2.JvsiZ3i/MsXTfsf9VItR8Gitg.GWgv7
mango	$2a$10$TFKgAYZrfb7p/J6Mz1NZsuhlp62Sa24GKBb7G8q4j702rc1Ntlopa
diaper	$2a$10$/ISCPiQC5wGh4JF9bXKJmel9OKvWdikq8cUuKmXvh5Za9HWcOADVy
tube	$2a$10$IkZSe0Y1h710V4JGV5hBD.ZVttOnizitpqdeu1nQvO7txdemlvta2
cloth	$2a$10$et.LBm.NeYWXhVI/TFB3cOsOkRAPFh8IBJSicap1ZUYNBqFlOLUp2
hair	$2a$10$6taHB2eQJDLeUUYL7Fw.O.u1avLILkOt74Jhv1uBHv350QAvwKRgC
smell	$2a$10$nVJwlzP5yheetOa8ALQGBehoreNsfY7eyC4X76tl3ZdiCGYtHNg4m
tip	$2a$10$xeKdWclook9IOKjcQO2GkOpzgPo.pkbc3QVIFsGKfv6UqYV2KoZIG
right	$2a$10$YOpfFI08OWinGu1/1T7NIIeGLsE1ey9ygq7.klvolS2jkz5MpjZfZu
wrong	$2a$10$6Q34ws6flQDvZU6RfttuaJeWC40c8GCO2NeZfmCHyoW7aZv9H1sYG2
eyes	$2a$10$vlcnd/G9fyDYVkIgvRhTUuTw26L57nw4MuZEYqHv2dSYiyppCnbA.
happy	$2a$10$3c3IF6ALH4kab4Cd8Zeq5OJEfSF9EcOcVJlxL5Ra.x9g8OVCjKKti

The way we typically protect against dictionary attacks is through employing a salt in our password encryption. Using a salt means that the attacker cannot just employ a standard encryption algorithm to generate the hash, but also needs to compute the hash with the associated salt.

Reverse Lookup Tables

Taking the process of dictionary attacks a bit further, and thus reducing time to decrypt, a reverse table stores the plain-text variation of a password beside the associated hash of the password in a table. The table is stored to be searched on the hash as opposed to the plain-text password.

If we go back to our dictionary attack list, it would look very similar, as shown in Table 2-2.

Table 2-2. Example lookup table

Hash	Associated word
$2a$10$wkmirMIMsQxpSvKpn.KNyOTU65YuneDcMXwA7XEHR5brjhpjugWCm	test
$2a$10$6Q34ws6flQDvZU6RfttuaJeWC40c8GCO2NeZfmCHyoW7aZv9H1sYG2	wrong

We start with obtaining the hashed password from the user record. We then compare that hash to the other hashes in our database. If there is a match, we pull the associated plain-text word for the password.

Like dictionary attacks, salting a password during hashing makes reverse lookup tables essentially useless. Even if the salts were obtained in a user information data breach, a lookup table would need to be generated for each word with the associated one-time-use salt, making it incredibly inefficient.

Rainbow Tables

There is typically much confusion over the difference between a rainbow table and a simple lookup table that stores a hash to a matching plain-text password. *Rainbow tables* are essentially a way of reducing the amount of storage needed to calculate a long list of password guesses to try in order to break a hash.

Let's compare that space/time trade-off. A rainbow table attack takes less processing time than a brute-force attack, but uses more storage. On the flip side, a rainbow table needs more processing time than a simple lookup table, but requires far less memory.

One important aspect is required for rainbow tables to function, and that's called a *reduction function*. In short, the purpose of a reduction function is to take a given hash and run the algorithm to generate the next possible plain-text password for us.

For instance, say the passwords that we are looking for are numeric, and a maximum of five digits in length. Our reduction function can have an algorithm that pulls the first five digits from the resulting hash, like so:

1. We start with arbitrary password 12345.
2. We use bcrypt to hash that password, giving us a hash of $2a$06$qEMn/vmty3PCCc5qxyOpOOjbJYnokP9zfwWVxT1jnfJqIQwOzuqjq.
3. We use our reduction function to take the first five characters we find in the hash.
4. That gives us the next plain-text password to try, 20635 (the literal first five numbers we encounter in the hash).

Here's how this whole process works in detail. Let's say we want to generate 10,000 potential plain-text passwords, and their associated hashes, to compare against hashes that we have from a compromised list of user records. If we were using a lookup table, we would have each of those plain-text passwords mapped directly to its hash. That requires a lot of storage, but is rather trivial to query to see if we have a match.

Here's how a rainbow table stores a chain of plain-text passwords and their associated hashes:

1. We take some arbitrary password, such as treehouse.
2. We then hash that, say with bcrypt, to give us a resulting hash, $2a$06$TjlWuN71X8Gsh031hK8qVueHhV4nsTi9ZGxk9fBSxwiU49nBw8kVy.
3. We then run that hash through our reduction function, giving us our next viable plain-text password.
4. Next, we repeat steps 2 and 3 for a lengthy number of chains, say 10,000.

Here's the secret. We store only the first plain-text password, and the last hash in the 10,000 word/hash chain. What we have done is created a list of 10,000 plain-text/hash-pair guesses, while storing only one plain-text password, and one hash.

 A rainbow table is not a decoding system for a hash, as hashing is built to be one-way (can encode but not decode). A hashing function allows you to map a plain-text password to a resulting hash, but if you try to get a plain-text password back from a hash, you'll get only some other random plain-text password. A rainbow table works in reverse, mapping a hash to its associated plain-text password. We aren't decoding; we're mapping.

Let's say we now have a hash that we want to get the plain-text password for. We follow a few steps to try to get it:

1. We look through the list of hashes that we have stored in our table (that last hash of a 10,000 word/hash chain). If we find a match, we just grab the associated word for that hash that we already precalculated.
2. If there is no match, we move to the next hash in the chain, hash #9,999, and do the same thing.
3. We then follow this process all the way to the end of the chain, tryng to find the associated plain-text password.

In a realistic implementation, we would have a multitude of chains created that we could run through. With multiple machines, we would run these chains in parallel to reduce the amount of time it would take to process the attack.

The best way to combat this attack is, again, through salting. In the case of attack vectors like this, having a long, complex password becomes important because:

- It takes exponentially more time to run these attacks with each additional character added.

- Parrot and parrot (change of case) need to be stored as different attack cases in the table, because they contain different characters. Adding mixed cases and special characters through the salt allows us to increase the size of the character set, and thus potential guesses, that an attacker needs to run through.

With that said, let's look at the process of salting in more depth to truly understand how to properly implement it in our hashing functions.

Salting

A *salt* is a sort of random data that is used in conjunction with the user password, when hashing, to harden the data and to protect against a few of our attack vectors, specifically dictionary attacks and rainbow tables. By providing that piece of random data, of significant length, we're ensuring that the produced hash is unique, so even if multiple users have the same password (as we know they do), the unique salt applied to the hash will ensure that the resulting hash itself is unique. The unique hash is what protects us from the hash comparison methodologies behind rainbow tables and dictionary attacks.

Let's look at this in practice. First, let's start by seeing what a hash might look like if we run it through scrypt with no applied salt. Let's assume the password that the user is using is mechagodzilla:

```
//example hashes using the password 'mechagodzilla' and no salt
hash('mechagodzilla') =
    162e0a91026a28f1f2afa11099d1fcbdd9f2e351095ebb196c90e10290ef1227
```

Each time scrypt hashes that password, the resulting hash will remain the same. If mechagodzilla is part of the word list tested through a dictionary attack, then it would be an easy matter of comparing the hashes and figuring out the user password.

Now let's see what applying a random salt to the equation will give us. Let's use the same mechagodzilla user password, but use a salt generated from the Node crypto library when the hash is created. Here are three instances of that at work:

```
//example hashes using the password 'mechagodzilla' and random salt
hash('mechagodzilla' + '458cf2979ef27397db670777775225334') =
    f3499a916612e285612b32702114751f557a70606c32b54b92de55153d40d3b6
hash('mechagodzilla' + 'ef5b72eff781b09a0784438af742dd6e') =
    7e29c5c48f44755598dec3549155ad66f1af4671091353be4c4d7694d71dc866
hash('mechagodzilla' + 'cc989b105a1c6a5f0fb460e29dd272f3') =
    6dedd3dbb0639e6e00ca0bf6272c141fb741e24925cb7548491479a1df2c215e
```

In simple terms, a salt of sufficient length and randomness provides a massive boost in security toward certain attack vectors, with just that simple, unique addition.

Generating a Random Salt

Let's look at how to generate a random salt for our hash functions by using the Node crypto library. Because it is part of the standard library, we don't have to go through the additional step of installing from npm.

The Node crypto library, in addition to providing functionality for generating random salts of varying length, also has built-in functionality for working with PBKDF2 to generate required hashes from the user password and salt.

We start by adding the crypto requirement to our Node project:

```
var crypto = require('crypto');
```

With that in place, we can generate our salt by using the randomBytes(…) method, like so:

```
crypto.randomBytes(32, function(ex, salt){
    //log readable string version of the salt
    console.log('salt: ' + salt.toString('hex'));

    //proceed to next step: using the salt
});
```

Generating a Salt Synchronously

Generating a salt via randomBytes can also be done synchronously, like so: var buf = crypto.randomBytes(256);.

The randomBytes method will accept a parameter for the size of the generated salt, in bytes. What is returned to us is the randomly generated salt. At this point, we can go to the next step of adding that salt to one our our hash functions, as we'll see in "Choosing the Right Password Hashing Function" on page 35.

Salt Reuse

One of the common issues in password hashing is reusing the salt over and over again. This completely defeats the purpose of using a salt to begin with. If we have a common salt being used, and a series of users who are using the same password, then the resulting hash will be the same. From there, an attacker can create a reverse lookup table and run a dictionary attack on each hash at the same time. When users create a new account, or they change their password, a new salt and hash should be generated and stored.

Salt Length

What is the appropriate length for our salt, and what are the implications of using a salt that is too short? Let's tackle the first part: what is the ideal length of the salt? One general rule of thumb is for the salt to be the same size as the output of the hash function used. If we look at SHA-256, for instance, the resulting hash is 32 bytes in length, so our salt should be 32 bytes, at minimum. In the case of SHA-1, the output length is 20 bytes, so our salt should be 20 bytes as well.

The PBKDF2 standard recommends that a salt length of at least 64 bits (8 bytes) be used to be effective.[4] In many cases, the next power of 2, so 128 bits (16 bytes), is typically used.

Let's move on to the implications of a using a short salt. If the generated salt is short, lookup tables can be created with all possible salt values and then be used to crack the data.

Where to Store the Salt

The first thought that you may have is that the salt should be stored in a secure location, separate from the hash. The simple fact is that we use the salt to prevent precomputed attacks (e.g., rainbow tables), where we would have a series of hashes that can be compared against what is stored in the user database. If we can prevent that easy/quick lookup from happening, we force the attacker to start cracking the hashes individually, which is significantly slower.

Because that is the case, we don't need to obfuscate or encrypt the salt, and it can be stored as a plain-text value in our database along with the hash. With that said, we also don't want to make it readily accessible (like a username) to the open world.

Peppering

One of the other concepts in password crytography, beyond the salt, is the concept of a pepper. Much like the salt, a *pepper* is another value that is added to the salt and password when hashing.

Where the salt and pepper differ is that instead of the pepper being stored alongside the hash (like a public key), and being randomly generated anew for each hash, the pepper is a more safeguarded key, and is typically pulled from a single, or subset, of strings.

The simple formula for pepper use is as follows:
```
hash(salt + pepper + password) = password hash
```

---

4 *https://tools.ietf.org/html/rfc2898#section-4.1*

When using a pepper, we will generally be following one of two scenarios:

- The pepper value is held in a different location than the password hash, and is treated more like a private key than a public key.

- The pepper is never stored, but is instead randomly chosen from a subset of values when the hash is generated. When doing a password comparison, we will instead compare the hash to the proposed password, the salt, and each possible value of the pepper, so we will make multiple comparisons against possible values for the pepper until the comparison either passes of fails. This means that the values for the pepper are calculated from the code layer, instead of the stored value.

In general, the reason to use a pepper is that the added characters and symbols can be utilized to bolster a weak password. By prepending a unique value that is chosen for a secure approach, we can harden passwords that would otherwise be easily crackable. Our password length is now increased, it has special characters, etc. With this, the resulting hash will be increasingly unique, helping to prevent dictionary attacks.

In reality, though, peppers have a few controversial aspects. Here are some of the reasons peppers are not heavily employed:

- A pepper is valuable only if it's kept secret. If an SQL injection attack is used, and only one table with the hash and salt are stolen, but the pepper is safe, then it does its job. Unfortunately, in many cases, the entire database structure is compromised and leaked, meaning that our pepper usually goes right along with it.

- Hashing algorithms that are employed en masse, and publicly vetted, do not accept a pepper as an argument. Most implementers can bring about some disastrous results by doing this wrong, or modifying the hashing algorithm, which is heavily discouraged.

- There is really no analysis of the benefits of a pepper out there, unlike salting.

Many in the cryptography community simply state that a salt of proper uniqueness and length, and a hash with an appropriate number of iterations employed to slow down cracking, is more than sufficient to make the pepper fairly useless.

In the end, it's good to understand that these mechanisms are out there, but in practice, it's sometimes more trouble than it's worth, especially when implementing proper hashing and salting.

Choosing the Right Password Hashing Function

Now that we understand how everything works, let's move on to how we are going to pick the hashing function that is best for our needs.

We already know that the three main hashing functions that we should be using for passwords are bcrypt, PBKDF2, and scrypt, but what's the difference between the three? Let's break these down a little bit further and explore the benefits of each, and how they are used in conjunction with a salt.

bcrypt

bcrypt is the first hashing function on our list. It's a key derivation function designed for passwords, and is based on the blowfish cipher.

Some of the benefits of bcrypt are as follows:

- It's based on the blowfish cipher, which uses RAM-based lookup tables that are constantly being altered throughout the execution of the algorithm. These types of tables are easy to handle for a CPU, but because of the sequential memory access and parallel processing required, the GPU falls short. In this way, it hinders GPU hardware enhancements by an attacker.
- It's specifically designed as a password hashing algorithm, with the intent of being slow (a good thing in password hashing).

With that in mind, let's jump into implementing this into our application or website.

First, we need to install the bcrypt package from npm, like so:

```
npm install bcrypt --save
```

We then require bcrypt in our Node app:

```
var bcrypt = require('bcrypt');
```

The bcrypt package has a built-in method for generating a salt, so we're going to be using that instead of the one that is made available in the crypto library, so that we don't need to include both bcrypt and crypto in our library:

```
function bcrypt_encrypt(username, password){
    bcrypt.genSalt(10, function(err, salt) {
        bcrypt.hash(password, salt, function(err, key) {
            //store username, hashed password, and salt in your database
        });
    });
}
```

We've built a function that accepts a username and password, presumably from user input when users are creating or updating their account. We're taking an asynchronous approach to generating the hash, which is the preferred method. We call `bcrypt.genSalt(…)` to create our salt. The method accepts the number of rounds (or cost) of the process (default is 10), and the callback to the method returns any error and the derived salt.

Once the salt is generated, we then call the `bcrypt.hash(…)` method to generate our hash. It will accept the password to be hashed and the salt we just generated. The callback will return the hash key that is generated from the process.

We can then take that hash and store it in our database along with the salt and the rest of the user record.

To do the same thing using a synchronous approach, we can do the following:

```
var salt = bcrypt.genSaltSync(10);
var hash = bcrypt.hashSync(password, salt);
```

PBKDF2

Next, let's look into *PBKDF2*, which is a key derivation function that has an academic background, coming from RSA laboratories.

PBKDF2 has a number of main benefits and implementations in the wild:

- Time tested and has been the subject of intense research over the years
- Recommended by NIST special publication 800-132[5]
- Used by password management systems 1Password, LastPass, and others
- Available as a standard method within the native Node crypto library

Because PBKDF2 is the hashing algorithm baked into the Node crypto library, it's fairly easy to get started. We first need to require crypto in our Node application:

```
var crypto = require('crypto');
```

Now, we build a function much as we did with bcrypt, to accept a username and password:

```
function pbkdf2_encrypt(username, password){
    crypto.randomBytes(32, function(ex, salt){
        crypto.pbkdf2(password, salt, 4096, 512, 'SHA-256', function(err, key) {
            if (err) throw err;
            //store username, hashed password, and salt in your database
        });
    });
}
```

We make a request to `crypto.randomBytes(…)` to generate a random salt for us. The method accepts the number of bytes of data to be generated (in our case, 32 bytes), and returns a salt.

---

5 *http://nvlpubs.nist.gov/nistpubs/Legacy/SP/nistspecialpublication800-132.pdf*

We then make a request to `crypto.pbkdf2(…)`, passing in the following:

- The user password.
- The salt.
- The number of iterations, or the number of times that the hash function should be applied (in our case, 4096).
- The keylength (in our case, 512).
- The digest function (in our case, SHA-256). You can get a list of supported digest functions with `crypto.getHashes()` (*http://bit.ly/crypto-gethashes*).

What is returned to us is a hex string containing our hash. We can push it to a plain string for viewing, like so:

```
console.log('key: ' + key.toString('hex'));
```

As before, we then store our username, hash, and salt in the user database.

To do the same thing synchronously:

```
const salt = crypto.randomBytes(32);
var result = crypto.pbkdf2Sync(password, salt, 4096, 512, 'SHA-256');
```

scrypt

Last on our hashing function list is *scrypt*. While there are many heated debates on the use of PBKDF2 versus bcrypt, and which is better, scrypt takes a very different approach to hashing than either of the two.

Benefits and implementations of scrypt include the following:

- Specifically designed to make it hardware and memory intensive for an attacker to perform large-scale attacks.
- Implemented as the algorithm behind the cryptocurrencies Litecoin and Dogecoin.

The main benefit here is that, unlike bcrypt and PBKDF2, scrypt is designed to be incredibly hardware and memory intensive in order to crack. In the case of bcrypt and PBKDF2, an attacker would be able to run thousands of parallel attacks on the hashed data from minimal hardware resources, since they are not meant to have large resource demands.

Let's get into the implementation. First, let's install scrypt using npm:

```
npm install scrypt --save
```

With scrypt, we're going to use a mix of the crypto library (for the salt), and the scrypt module (for the hash). We include those two into our Node application like this:

```
var scrypt = require('scrypt'),
    crypto = require('crypto');
```

With everything in place, we again have a function that accepts a username and password:

```
function scrypt_encrypt(username, password){
    crypto.randomBytes(32, function(ex, salt){
        scrypt.hash(password, {"N":16384,"r":8,"p":1}, 64, salt,
            function(err, key) {
                //store username, hashed password, and salt
                //in your database
            }
        );
    });
}
```

We use the crypto library to generate our salt, with crypto.randomBytes(…), passing in the number of bytes that should be generated in the output. The output gives us the generated salt.

We then go to our next step of generating the hash with that salt. We make a request to scrypt.hash(…), which accepts a number of values:

- The user password to be hashed.
- An object containing the parameters to control the scrypt hashing:
  — N: The maximum amount of time in seconds that scrypt will spend computing the derived key (double).
  — r: The maximum number of bytes of RAM used when computing the derived key (integer). The default is 0.
  — p: The fraction of the available RAM used when computing the derived key (0 to 1, converted to percentages). The default is 0.5.
- The length of the resulting hash.
- The salt we just generated.

Once computed, the derived hash will be sent back for us to store.

The same approach synchronously would look like this:

```
const salt = crypto.randomBytes(256);
var result = scrypt.hashSync(key,{"N":16384,"r":8,"p":1}, 64, salt);
```

Validating a Password Against a Hashed Value

Once we have a hashed valued of a password stored with the salt in our database, how do we validate that the hash we have stored matches a login attempt by a user at future iterations of the application use?

Because we are working with one-way hash functions, there is a simple way to validate a hash against another password to see if they are valid. We just follow a few steps:

1. We capture the password from the user login attempt.

2. We look up the record from our database that matches who the user is purporting to be, and get the hash and the salt.

3. We use the same hashing function that we did to derive that hash (e.g., bcrypt) with the salt from the database, to generate a new hash.

4. We compare the newly generated hash with the hash from the database. If they match, we have a valid password.

If we follow that process for PBKDF2, we can see how the comparison will work:

```
var dbsalt = 'USER RECORD SALT FROM YOUR DATABASE';
var dbhash = 'USER RECORD KEY FROM YOUR DATABASE';

crypto.pbkdf2(password, dbsalt, 4096, 512, 'SHA-256', function(err, comparehash){
    if (err) throw err;
    if (dbhash.toString('hex') === comparehash.toString('hex')){
        //passwords match
    } else {
        //passwords don't match
    }
});
```

As you can see, the preceding code looks quite similar to the encryption process with PBKDF2. There are several things that we need to note about the comparison process:

- We first capture the hash and salt from our local user record storage for the user who is trying to log in (variables dbsalt and dbhash).

- We then encrypt the password for the login attempt (the password that the user supplied to log in) and encrypt it using dbsalt, the same salt that encrypted the user password during registration.

- Once that hash is produced (the comparehash variable), we then compare the hash stored for that user in their user record (dbhash) against the newly generated version.

- If the password was the same, using the same salt to encrypt the password and compare against the stored value, then we will have a matching password and can safely log the user in.

Some packages, such as bcrypt, make that process a bit easier for us by providing a compare method. The compare method simplifies the steps of having to encrypt the password with the salt that we stored by mixing hashing and comparison into a single call, like so:

```
bcrypt.compare(password, hash, function(err, res) {
    //returns true or false
});
```

In this case, we're supplying the raw user password from the login attempt and the hash from the database. The result will be either `true` or `false`, depending on whether they're a match.

Key Stretching

One of the underlying concepts that makes bcrypt, scrypt, and PBKDF2 effective is a technique that they employ called *key stretching*. As we learned in Chapter 1, a vast majority of people don't utilize standards of significant password length and complexity to keep their profile data secure, and prevent attack vectors like brute-force attacks, on their own. This is where key stretching comes in. It takes a potentially weak password and outputs an encrypted key of significant length and complexity that attack vectors like brute forcing no longer become viable options.

In the case of our cryptographic hash functions, key stretching is done by applying the hash function repeatedly in a loop, until a hash of the desired length and complexity is obtained. When we talked about number of iterations in the hash function examples previously, that is the implementation of this key-stretching concept.

Recomputing Hashes

At some point, you may have the need to generate new secure password hashes for your users. Perhaps:

- Hardware has changed because of Moore's law and you need to change the weight/work factor used by your encryption algorithms.
- Algorithms have changed, and the one you are using is no longer secure, or something better has come along.
- The hashes are no longer as secure as they can be.

In these instances, the standard practice is to store a new hash for the users as they use your system. As each user logs in with their username/password, you log them in as you normally would by comparing the login hash with the stored hash. Then, instead of throwing out the password, you generate a new hash for the user, and replace the old one in the user database record, before throwing out the password.

To speed this process along, you can force logout for all users. For instance, if you allow users to remain logged in via a session cookie, you can invalidate all user cookies and force each user to log in on their next visit.

Next Steps

Expanding upon the concepts of password security, Chapter 3 looks at a few practical approaches to protecting our systems against attack vectors.

CHAPTER 3

Identity Security Fundamentals

Tim Messerschmidt and Jonathan LeBlanc

After discussing the ongoing issues with current security models in the first chapter and introducing secure passwords, hashing, and salting in the second chapter, we now focus on using a person's identity across multiple sites to handle different authentication and authorization scenarios.

Merriam-Webster defines *identity* as "the qualities, beliefs, etc., that make a particular person or group different from others." These qualities are what make identity relevant to the concept of security.

Understanding Various Identity Types

While using the Internet, an individual establishes an *online identity* that represents certain elements or characteristics of that person. This form of identity can—and often will—differ across multiple sites and leads to a fragmentation that we can group into different areas based on a website's use case.

In this section, we introduce three types of identity that we will then discuss in detail: social identity, concrete identity, and thin identity. These types of identity often overlap and can share the same attributes, as shown in Figure 3-1.

These three identity types can be considered *federated identities* and are applied through technologies such as SAML, OpenID, OAuth, and tokenization. Often applied through single sign-on—known as SSO—Federated Identity Management (FIM or FIdM) is the practice of using a set of identity attributes across multiple systems or organizations. While SSO is a way of using the same credentials across multiple sites and applications, FIM shifts the verification of credentials toward the identity provider.

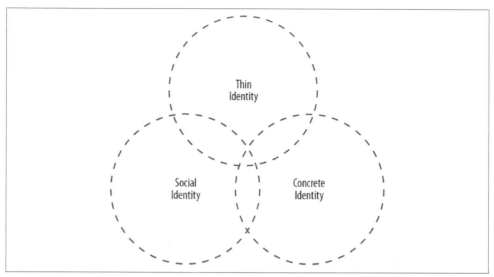

Figure 3-1. Overlapping identities

Social Identity

Social identity came up with the rise of social networks and can be seen as a very moderate form of identity that people tend to share quite casually. Profile information often concentrates on social connections, interests, and hobbies, while ignoring or not necessarily favoring critical information that might be used against the user.

Services such as Facebook or Google+ allow users to quickly access other services by using their already populated profiles and leverage scopes in order to control the level of information shared. This quickly became a favored way of handling login scenarios, especially on mobile phones, because it provides a big boost in convenience and helps to avoid the issues of entering any kind of complex information on touchscreens.

Concrete Identity

Leveraging social identity is completely valid and even encouraged for services such as games, media consumption, and of course, social networks. But other use cases such as online banking or ecommerce require a more concrete profile that provides useful information—for example, the user's email, address, phone number, spoken languages, or age.

Especially in ecommerce scenarios, the payment process can be painful. Having to enter a 16+ digit credit card number manually can be tedious on a physical device and troublesome on a touchscreen. This is where services such as PayPal, Amazon Payments, or Google Wallet come in. These services enable users to enter valuable information in one place, and reuse it on multiple sites. By tokenizing sensible credentials such as payment details, the checkout flow is sped up tremendously.

Another popular example of using *concrete identity* is in the election process and many other state services. For example, in Lithuania, a citizen's state-issued ID card is backed up by OpenID.[1] This enables a form of eGovernment that allows people living remotely to participate in ongoing discussions and actively contribute to the country's politic environment.

Thin Identity

Thin identity is an old concept that is currently gaining popularity again. Thin identity—or even *no* identity—simply means user authentication without gaining access to profile information.

A good example is Twitter's service Digits (*http://get.digits.com*), which allows users to use their phone number as a means of logging in. The identifying—and globally unique—bit here is the person's phone number. Looking at the definition of *identity* introduced at the beginning of this chapter, the criterion of difference (from other phone numbers) is certainly met. Digits and other similar services aim to replace error-prone and vulnerable passwords with another factor that seems to be universally given. Yahoo! went a similar route and provided a way to do passwordless login using text messages with one-time-only passwords[2]—this is not yet part of Yahoo!'s developer offerings, though.

Enhancing User Experience by Utilizing Identity

User experience studies carried out by the Nielsen Norman Group show that login doesn't necessarily have to be the first point of contact for users and often harms the conversion process of turning visitors into users by forcing them to register or log in.[3] The current sentiment in user-experience research is that a preview of offered functionality is desirable and helps people decide whether they want to commit to an application.

Leveraging existing profiles, such as a user's social identity, can help ease the way after the user does decide to register by prepopulating profile information and therefore lowering the amount of information the user has to type in manually.

---

1 *http://lists.openid.net/pipermail/openid-eu/2009-February/000280.html*

2 *http://www.infopackets.com/news/9545/new-yahoo-login-system-uses-no-password*

3 *https://www.nngroup.com/articles/login-walls*

Introducing Trust Zones

The devices we use nowadays come pre-equipped with a variety of sensors that can gather information about the user's environment. GPS, WiFi, cameras, accelerometers, gyroscopes, light, and many other sensors are used to build up profiles and identify the user accordingly. Combining this concept with the concept of identity, we can not only identify users, but also build up trust zones (Figure 3-2).

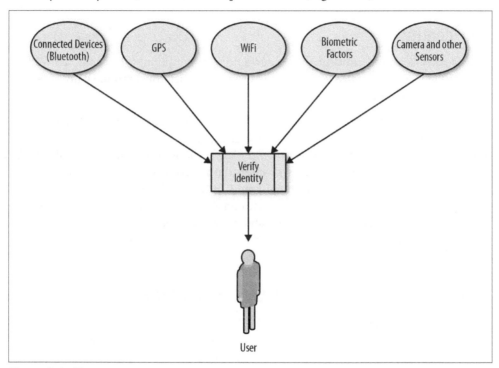

Figure 3-2. Trust zones

Trust zones allow us to scale our security based on users' behavior, environment, and our ability to determine whether they are who they say they are. In essence, we are trying to create a digital fingerprint for the user, from any data that might be available and unique for the given user, such as their browser configuration, hardware, devices, location, etc.

If we can guarantee a user is at home, based on the current GPS coordinates and the WiFi used to connect to the Internet, trust zones can offer the user a way to waive certain steps within authorization and authentication of web and mobile applications.

Google introduced this concept for Android as a feature known as Smart Lock.[4] When a user wears his Android Wear device, the phone can be set up to automatically unlock whenever a Bluetooth connection between the wearable device and the user's phone is established.[5] Other supported factors for Smart Lock are the user's location, face recognition, and on-body detection, which is a feature that relies on the device's accelerometer. Chapter 5 covers these alternate ways of user authentication more deeply.

Realistically, we're trying to remove hurdles during the application experience for the users. If we can obtain enough bits of information about them from the system and devices that they are using to determine that they are almost certainly who they say they are, and they are in a trusted location, is it necessary to challenge them when changing account information, or ask them to provide login details during a checkout process instead of providing a one-click checkout experience?

These are the types of things that we can do when we have a strong certainty that users are who they are purporting to be.

Let's take this conversation into a practical look at this technology, starting with the browser.

Browser Fingerprinting

One of our main goals as application and web developers is to make the experience of our users as secure and as convenient as possible. With the concept of trust zones understood, you can start to see how many of the security measures that we can put in place may occur without burdening the user for more information.

One of the methods that can be employed is *browser fingerprinting*. This process uses unique characteristics about the browser that the user is using, such as headers, fonts, etc., to determine a second factor of authentication based on the user's browser.

Back in May of 2010, The Electronic Frontier Foundation (EFF) (*https://www.eff.org*) published a report from an experiment it was running on browser fingerprinting, called Panopticlick (*https://panopticlick.eff.org*). From this study, some interesting results were derived from the browsers that were tested during the first 1 million visits to the Panopticlick site.[6]

- 84% of browsers tested had a unique configuration.
- Among browsers that had Flash or Java installed, 94% were unique.

---

4 *http://developers.google.com/identity/smartlock-passwords/android*

5 *http://support.google.com/nexus/answer/6093922?hl=en*

6 *https://www.eff.org/deeplinks/2010/05/every-browser-unique-results-fom-panopticlick*

- Only 1% had fingerprints that were seen more than twice.

These are obviously not definitive numbers to determine to a near certainty the browser uniqueness of each user, but the numbers are significant enough to be able to easily use these types of tests as a second factor of authentication for our users. When we are able to find a unique browser configuration, we have a high likelihood (99%) of determining that the browser is unique and attributable to that individual. When using this, coupled with additional techniques that we will explore in later sections, we can predict with a high degree of certainty that users are who they say they are. When we have that determination, along with the login mechanisms that the user has used (such as a username/password), then we are able to maintain a high level of confidence to create our trust zones.

These tests used the concept of *bits of entropy* to determine the fingerprint of a browser. From its subset of tests, the EFF noticed that the distribution of entropy observed on a tested browser is typically around 18.1 bits. This means that if a browser was chosen at random, at best we would expect that only 1 in 286,777 other browsers would share the same fingerprint.

In addition to making things easier for the user through these trust zones, there's another benefit to having this information tracked. If we are processing payments for our users, inevitably there will be some disputes over a payment and who may have made it. Being able to provide information such as these digital fingerprints during dispute resolution can help to provide favorable results during the process.

Configurations More Resistant to Browser Fingerprinting

In its study, the EFF also noticed that certain configurations had a high resistance to browser fingerprinting, meaning that they were harder to generate a fingerprint for. These configurations included the following:

- Browsers with JavaScript, or disabled plug-ins.
- Browsers with TorButton installed, which anticipated and defended against the fingerprinting techniques.
- Mobile devices, because the lack of configurability of the mobile browser tends to lead to a more generic fingerprint. These devices generally do not have good interfaces for controlling cookies, so information may be obtained more easily through that method.
- Corporate desktop machines that are precise clones of one another, and don't allow for degrees of configuration.
- Browsers running in anonymous mode.

Identifiable Browser Information

Through the studies that were performed during the Panopticlick project, the EFF was able to assign different entropy bit levels for different configuration types that can be derived from a browser. These included the characteristics and associated entropy values listed in Table 3-1.

Table 3-1. Entropy (bits) for browser characteristics

Characteristic	Bits of entropy
User Agent	10.0
Plug-ins	15.4
Fonts	13.9
Video	4.83
Supercookies	2.12
HTTP ACCEPT Header	6.09
Time Zone	3.04
Cookies Enabled	0.353

The browser uniqueness report, in addition to providing the characteristics, also provided the means through which those values were obtained,[7] as shown in Table 3-2.

Table 3-2. How browser characteristics were obtained

Characteristic	Method
User Agent	This was transmitted via HTTP, and logged by the server. It contains the browser micro-version, OS version, language, toolbar information, and other information on occasion.
Plug-ins	The PluginDetect (*http://www.pinlady.net/PluginDetect*) JavaScript library was used to check eight common plug-ins. Extra code was also used to estimate the current version of Acrobat Reader. The data was then transmitted via AJAX post.
Fonts	A flash or Java applet was used, and the data was collected via JavaScript and transmitted via AJAX post.
HTTP ACCEPT Header	Transmitted by HTTP and logged by the server
Screen Resolution	JavaScript AJAX post.
Supercookies (partial test)	JavaScript AJAX post.
Time Zone	JavaScript AJAX post.
Cookies Enabled	Inferred in HTTP, and logged by the server.

---

7 *https://panopticlick.eff.org/static/browser-uniqueness.pdf*

Looking at a breakdown of all characteristics, we have a good idea of how to implement these techniques. For the most part, we're pulling data via JavaScript and logging on our server, and at most (in the case of fonts), we have a flash or Java applet doing the work for us.

Capturing Browser Details

Let's take a look at the methods that we can use to begin capturing some of this information from client-side JavaScript. This will be part of the data that we will need in order to start generating a fingerprint for our users, as they come through.

User agent

Let's start with a simple one, the user agent. This will provide us with quite a bit of information that we can use for the overall fingerprint.

To obtain this string, we can use the data within the `navigator` object, like so:

```
var agent = navigator.userAgent;
```

From this test, you may see a string returned that would look something like the following:

```
Mozilla/5.0 (Macintosh; Intel Mac OS X 10_10_5) AppleWebKit/537.36
(KHTML, like Gecko) Chrome/48.0.2564.116 Safari/537.36
```

There are some important pieces of information contained in this string that we can use. Specifically:

Mozilla/5.0
Mozilla-compatible user agent and version. This is used for historical reasons, and has no real meaning in modern browsers.

Intel Mac OS X 10_10_5
The operating system and version.

AppleWebKit/537.36
Web kit and build.

KHTML, like Gecko
Open source HTML layout engine (KHTML), like Gecko.

Chrome/48.0.2564.116
Browser (Chrome) and version.

Safari/537.36
Based on browser (Safari) and build.

Time zone

Next, let's capture the time zone by using `getTimezoneOffset()`. This function will return the offset, in minutes, from GMT. To obtain the number of hours that the user is offset from GMT, we can divide that result by 60, like so:

```
var offset = new Date().getTimezoneOffset() / 60;
```

You may notice something strange about the result here. The hour is correct, but the negative/positive identifier is flipped. For instance, if I am on the East Coast of the United States (GMT-5), the result returned is 5, not 5. This is because `getTimezoneOffset()` is calculating GMT's offsite from your time zone, not the other way around. If you wish to have it the other way around, multiply by –1, like so:

```
var offset = (new Date().getTimezoneOffset() / 60) * -1;
```

Screen resolution

The screen resolution can be obtained by using the `window` object. This will give us the screen resolution of the monitor being used, which can be a fairly static indicator for the browser fingerprint.

We can obtain those results with the following snippets:

```
var width = window.screen.width;
var height = window.screen.height;
```

This will give us the given numeric results for the width and height, such as 2560 (width) and 1440 (height) for a screen resolution of 2560 x 1440.

Plug-ins

Browser plug-in information can garner quite a bit of detail for the fingerprint, and is obtained via `navigator.plugins`. Let's say we want to capture the name of each plug-in installed in the browser, and just display those for the time being. We can do so with the following code:

```
//get plugin information
var plugins = navigator.plugins;
for (var i = 0; i < plugins.length; i++){
    console.log(plugins[i].name);
}
```

JavaScript Library for Plug-in Detection

An alternative method for obtaining additional plug-in information from the browser is through the PluginDetect JavaScript library (*http://www.pinlady.net/PluginDetect*).

The information displayed, depending on the plug-ins installed in the browser, may look something like the following:

```
Widevine Content Decryption Module
Chrome PDF Viewer
Shockwave Flash
Native Client
```

That information can be added to the custom identifiers for the user's browser.

Location-Based Tracking

Other than browser fingerprinting, another method that we can use for building trust zones for users is to use their physical location.

Here's how this can be valuable. Let's say that we have an ecommerce store where the user has filled out her shipping address during sign-up or a previous purchase. We have that address stored to make it easier for the user to check out, and that has become a trusted home location. If we could determine the physical location of the person attempting to use the site while purporting to be the user, we could match that against the address on file. If those two addresses match, we can use that as a trusted point, and potentially lift the need to have the user confirm her login information before checkout.

Use Geolocation with Caution

Use gelocation data from the user with caution. Physical location can be masked, and may provide inaccurate results. With that said, ensure that you use alternate methods of identification with geolocation, and use with caution.

Let's look at a simple JavaScript-based approach to gathering the latitude and longitude of the user, using the `navigator` object. First, let's see what the current support for geolocation is within modern browsers (Figure 3-3).

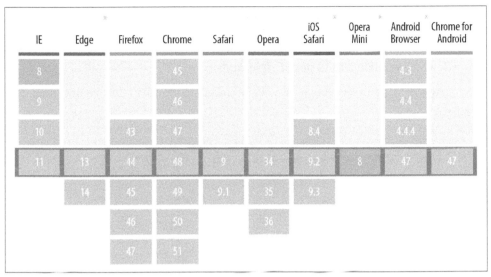

IE	Edge	Firefox	Chrome	Safari	Opera	iOS Safari	Opera Mini	Android Browser	Chrome for Android
8			45					4.3	
9			46					4.4	
10		43	47			8.4		4.4.4	
11	13	44	48	9	34	9.2	8	47	47
	14	45	49	9.1	35	9.3			
		46	50		36				
		47	51						

Figure 3-3. Current geolocation browser support

Looking at the support, we have good overall coverage in most modern browsers. Now let's see how to set up a simple example of this:

```
//on success handler
function success(position){
    console.log('lat: ' + position.coords.latitude);
    console.log('lon: ' + position.coords.longitude);
}

//error handler
function failure(err){
    console.log(err);
}

//check geolocation browser availability and capture coordinates
if ('geolocation' in navigator){
    navigator.geolocation.getCurrentPosition(success, failure, {timeout:10000});
} else {
    console.log('geolocation is not available');
}
```

We start out by defining two handler functions, one for success and the other for handling errors. Within the success function we will be passed position data, from which we can then extract coordinate information. Within the error handler, we are simply logging out the errors that may be produced. One potential error may be caused by the user not allowing the website to capture his geolocation:

```
PositionError {}
 - code: 1
 - message: "User denied Geolocation"
```

With those in place, we check at the bottom of the sample to see whether geolocation is available within the `navigator` object. If it is, we call `navigator.geolocation.get CurrentPosition(...)`, passing in the `success` function, `error` function, and the options, which contain a time-out of 10 seconds.

When run in a browser, the user will be asked to confirm his geolocation data (Figure 3-4).

Figure 3-4. Requesting use of geolocation data

Once allowed, we will be able to extract the latitude and longitude, compare those to the address we have stored on file, and see whether the user is in a trusted zone. Creating a geofence of an appropriate range (range from the root address that the coordinates are within) will allow us to handle cases of the user being within close proximity to his home location.

Other Methods

There are many other methods for obtaining geolocation information for a user. For instance, within a mobile application environment, we can leverage off of the GPS data for the same end result.

Device Fingerprinting (Phone/Tablet)

As you can see, a multitude of data points can be gathered to help us determine whether users are who they say they are, without impacting their experience. This allows us to continue to make things easier by not having to request additional information from them for security.

Another method is to use the hardware fingerprint of the devices that are being used by the person using our site or service. Users will typically use a range of devices (phones, tablets, etc.) for interacting with your applications. These devices, when used over time, can become trusted sources to help determine whether the user is on a trusted device.

Let's take a look at a simple method for capturing this type of information from an Android application. Build information is available that enable us to obtain information about the device that the user is using.[8]

Some of that information can be pulled like so:

```
//Build Info: http://developer.android.com/reference/android/os/Build.html

System.getProperty("os.version"); //os version
android.os.Build.DEVICE           //device
android.os.Build.MODEL            //model
android.os.Build.VERSION.SDK_INT  //sdk version of the framework
android.os.Build.SERIAL           //hardware serial number, if available
.
.
.
```

We can obtain information such as the OS version, device, and model. This can all go toward building a framework of trusted devices, and allowing a user to bypass the need for additional levels of security, should they be required.

Changing Devices

A typical question here may be, "What if I change my device?" If a device is changed, the system should note that the device is not trusted, and show appropriate security challenges as one would for an untrusted user. Once the user has verified her identity through the challenges, that device can then be added to the list of trusted devices.

Device Fingerprinting (Bluetooth Paired Devices)

Today our phones are not the only connected devices we have. We may have our phones connected to a smart watch, a car, or other hardware around us. These devices, much like the phone, can be used as a hardware fingerprint to help determine whether users are who they say they are. If we can find devices that are typically connected to the phone, the trust score would increase.

Let's look at an example of how this would work within an Android application, if we wanted to fetch all of the Bluetooth devices that are connected to a phone:

```
//fetch all bonded bluetooth devices
Set<BluetoothDevice> pairedDevices = mBluetoothAdapter.getBondedDevices();

//if devices found, fetch name and MAC address for each
if (pairedDevices.size() > 0){
```

---

8 *http://developer.android.com/reference/android/os/Build.html*

```
    for (BluetoothDevice device : pairedDevices){
        //Device Name - device.getName()
        //Device MAC address - device.getAddress()
    }
}
```

We start by calling `getBondedDevices()` to capture any devices that are currently attached to the phone. We then loop through the devices found, and can fetch some basic information about them:

Device name
> Readable name of the device, obtained through `device.getName()`

MAC address
> The physical address of the device, obtained through `device.getAddress()`

 Setting Proper Permissions

As of Android 6.0, there have been permission changes to provide users with greater data protection. In order to obtain hardware identifiers (such as the MAC address) of a Bluetooth-attached device, you need to set the `ACCESS_FINE_LOCATION` or `ACCESS_COARSE_LOCATION` permissions in your app. If those permissions are not set, `device.getAddress()` will return a constant value of 02:00:00:00:00:00.[9]

Implementing Identity

Now that you have built up an understanding of identity types and the concepts behind trust zones, in Chapter 4 we will take on a basic implementation of OAuth 2.0 and OpenID—the driving technologies behind identity. Please note that the identity sector is currently evolving, and new standards, such as FIDO, are on the horizon. These new technologies will be part of Chapter 5's focus.

---

9 *http://developer.android.com/about/versions/marshmallow/android-6.0-changes.html*

Securing the Login with OAuth 2 and OpenID Connect

Tim Messerschmidt

In this chapter, we discuss the concepts behind the two standards—*OAuth 2.0* and *OpenID Connect*—in order to provide a comprehensive overview of current authentication and authorization standards. To do so, the difference between authentication and authorization is outlined, followed by an explanation of OAuth's evolution throughout the years. Afterward, we sketch out a basic implementation of an OAuth 2.0 server and client that leverages OpenID Connect functionality.

The Difference Between Authentication and Authorization

A common issue is seeing authentication and authorization as one and the same. In fact, they are very different and can be used in different scenarios or combined to allow access to different kinds of information. This section provides a basic understanding of the main differences and discusses why multiple standards exist and are being pushed forward at the same time.

Authentication

Authentication is the process of identifying a user against a service. OpenID was the first standard that aimed at providing a decentralized protocol for identifying users across multiple sites. The idea behind this was very simple: avoiding the tedious task of re-entering information over and over. Basically the login process is being delegated to another site.

OpenID was introduced in 2005 and saw enormous growth, totaling over 1 billion user accounts in 2009.[1] Recent development showed less demand for OpenID and central identity platforms. Instead, hybrid approaches were being introduced that offered both user authentication and authorization at the same time.

Authorization

While authentication aims at user identity, *authorization* tries to solve the issue of providing access to a user's protected resources. This can involve providing access to user profiles—which blurs the line between authentication and authorization—or simple anomynous access to data.

Authorization standards like OAuth are often used as a more convenient and more secure way of handling sign-in than regular basic authentication flows using usernames and passwords. Authorization relies on third-party authentication systems and is often used for various social login scenarios using service providers like Facebook, Google+, or Twitter.

What Are OAuth and OpenID Connect?

The first draft of the OAuth 1.0 Core (*http://oauth.net/core/1.0*) was released in December 2007. The idea behind OAuth was to provide an authentication technology that would allow for anonymous resource sharing with third parties. Anonymous resource sharing can be seen as a way of providing access to information and resources without the need to provide information about the user's identity.

In the OAuth process, the server side is referred to as the Service Provider, and the client is called the Consumer. In order to allow for resource sharing and accessing a user's protected resources, a process called *OAuth authorization flow* is initiated that consists of eight steps:

1. Consumer: Retrieve a Request Token
2. Service Provider: Grant Request Token

---

1 *http://openid.net/2009/12/16/openid-2009-year-in-review/*

3. Consumer: Direct user to the Service Provider in order to sign in

4. Service Provider: Obtain authorization

5. Service Provider: Redirect the user to the Consumer

6. Consumer: Request an Access Token

7. Service Provider: Grant Access Token

8. Consumer: Use Access Token to access protected resources

This flow—as outlined in the official specification—is known as *three-legged OAuth*. Three-legged OAuth requires using a web browser to obtain a user's authorization. The three parties involved in the process are as follows:

1. The Consumer (which we also identify as the Client)

2. The Service Provider

3. The End User

The whole reason for this convoluted process comes from the desire to prevent the Consumer from ever handling the user's credentials (username and password). By involving all three parties, only a minimum of information is provided in order to grant access to a User's resources. By implementing OAuth, a potentially insecure password is replaced by an opaque token that can be revoked by the application and the End User. This results in avoiding the password anti-pattern.

> Users should have access to their data and should be allowed to bring it from one site to another. Social sites shouldn't propagate bad behavior by teaching users that it's OK to give any site their usernames and passwords for all the sites to which they belong.[2]
>
> —Designing Social Interfaces

An alternative flow, known as *two-legged OAuth* (Figure 4-1), skips obtaining the user's authorization because no user data is being requested or involved. User data can be filled within the Consumer and stored afterward within the Service Provider. The two-legged OAuth flow can be used as a replacement for traditional basic authentication.

---

2 *http://designingsocialinterfaces.com/patterns/The_Password_Anti-Pattern*

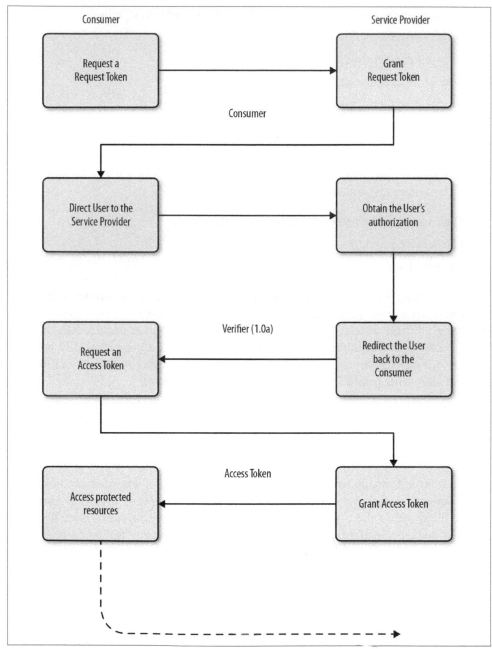

Figure 4-1. OAuth 1.0a authorization flow

The Internet Engineering Task Force (IETF) started supporting OAuth in November 2008. The official Request for Comments was published in 2010.[3]

OAuth 1.0a

Revision 1.0a of OAuth was released in June 2009. It serves as a hotfix for possible session fixation attacks that allowed access to the victim's resources.

Eran Hammer, one of the coauthors of OAuth 1.0, wrote a blog post about the possible exploit and how OAuth 1.0a fixes this attack vector.[4]

In this book we use OAuth 1.0a as a base for any discussion regarding the first version of OAuth.

From a security perspective, the first version of OAuth relies heavily on signing the request on the Consumer's side using HMAC-SHA1, RSA-SHA1, or PLAINTEXT. A Service Provider is allowed to implement other signing methods. The signature is being passed as the oauth_signature parameter, while the method used to sign the signature is being provided via oauth_signature_method. Nonces and timestamps are being leveraged as additional security mechanisms that aim at avoiding replay attacks.

The process of signing requests and the bloated process of retrieving an Access Token are among the main reasons behind criticism for OAuth 1.0a. Developers often feel like they have to rely on libraries in order to implement OAuth 1.0-based authentication and feel like the standard is not approachable.

Introducing OAuth 2.0

Since the Web changed heavily and new form factors were released, new authentication scenarios had to be introduced in order to accommodate web applications, native applications for desktop and mobile, and even interfaceless Consumers such as Internet of Things devices. Furthermore, demand for more simplicity has been rising among the developer community. Both reasons led to the introduction of the first draft of OAuth 2.0 in April 2010.[5] The main framework for OAuth 2.0 RFC[6] and a RFC discussing OAuth 2.0 Bearer Token Usage[7] were published in 2012.

---

3 *http://tools.ietf.org/html/rfc5849*

4 *http://hueniverse.com/2009/04/23/explaining-the-oauth-session-fixation-attack*

5 *http://tools.ietf.org/html/draft-ietf-oauth-v2-01*

6 *http://tools.ietf.org/html/rfc6749*

7 *http://tools.ietf.org/html/rfc6750*

To address some of the main differences between OAuth 1.0a and 2.0, the following details were updated:

1. Access Tokens are now subject to a time to live (TTL)/expiry time.

2. No more client-side cryptography.

3. Different flows to accommodate different authentication scenarios.

Drama around OAuth 2.0

If you are aware of the ongoing discussion between the OAuth 2.0 stakeholders or you simply don't care, feel free to skip to the next section!

While OAuth 2.0 fixes a lot of the issues that OAuth 1.0 had, it is far from perfect and saw its biggest critique coming from Eran Hammer, who participated in the OAuth 2.0 working group. In a post called "OAuth 2.0 and the Road to Hell," Hammer writes about his frustration with a standard that often lacks concrete implementation strategies and leaves a lot of decision making to the implementer.[8] One of the points he touches on is that Bearer Tokens are not encrypted per se and therefore are inherently less secure than specified. OAuth 2.0 puts the trust into TLS and SSL and doesn't add additional security mechanisms on top of these protocols in order to control token ownership.

Other contributors, such as Tim Bray, on the other hand, raise valid points about OAuth 2.0 being usable already, working in its core, and not necessarily having the need for interoperability.

> Having said all that, OAuth 2 may not be perfect, and may have been harmed by the Enterprise crap, but the core of Web functionality (all I care about) seems to have survived.[9]
>
> —Tim Bray, "On the Deadness of OAuth 2"

---

8 *http://hueniverse.com/2012/07/26/oauth-2-0-and-the-road-to-hell*

9 *https://www.tbray.org/ongoing/When/201x/2012/07/28/Oauth2-dead*

OAuth 1.0 versus OAuth 2.0

Overall the industry seems to agree that OAuth 2.0 is a better standard than its predecessor by offering an easier implementation and more flexibility in terms of defining access to resources. Many developers are heavily challenged when implementing OAuth 1.0's signatures and often run into outdated or even deprecated libraries. When you are able to use secure connections (which we highly recommend and explain in Chapter 7), it makes sense to go for the slimmer OAuth 2.0—otherwise, we'd recommend taking a deeper look into OAuth 1.0a.

Looking at the tech landscape, there are only few active companies remaining that still build upon OAuth 1.0 (such as Evernote[10]). Twitter, another prominent implementer of OAuth 1.0a, nowadays offers a hybrid implementation that uses both OAuth 1.0a and OAuth 2.0[11] based on the API you wish to use. Google, on the other hand, announced that its OAuth 1.0 support has been deprecated as of April 20, 2012 and actively encourages developers to start using OAuth 2.0 instead.[12]

Handling Authorization with OAuth 2.0

In OAuth 2.0 the classical OAuth authorization flow, also known as the *OAuth dance*, was simplified in order to require fewer steps:

1. Consumer: Direct user to the Service Provider in order to sign in

2. Service Provider: Obtain authorization

3. Service Provider: Redirect the user to the Consumer

4. Consumer: Use Authorization Code to request Access Token

5. Service Provider: Grant Access Token

6. Consumer: Use Access Token to access protected resources

This flow is a very basic summary of the process that happens when users aim to authorize clients through OAuth 2.0. Figure 4-2 illustrates a more comprehensive version of the OAuth dance.

---

10 *http://dev.evernote.com/doc/articles/authentication.php*

11 *http://dev.twitter.com/oauth/reference/post/oauth2/token*

12 *https://developers.google.com/identity/protocols/OAuthForWebApps*

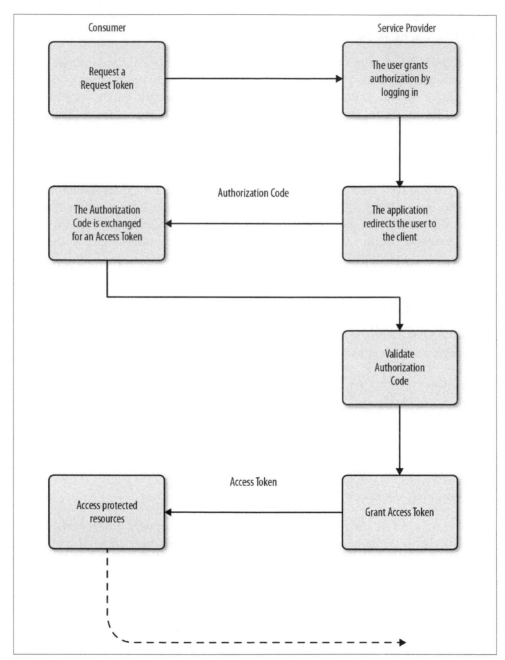

Figure 4-2. OAuth 2.0 authorization dance

OAuth 2.0 Authorization Grant Types

According to the specification, the various OAuth 2.0 Grant Types are defined as follows:

Authorization Code
> An intermediate token is being used to prevent sharing the resource owner's credentials

Implicit
> The client is not being authenticated

Resource Owner Password Credentials
> Used to obtain an authorization grant

Client Credentials
> When the client is also the resource owner

A less confusing translation is provided by Aaron Parecki:[13]

Authorization Code
> For apps running on a web server

Implicit
> For browser-based or mobile apps

Resource Owner Password Credentials
> For logging in with a username and password

Client Credentials
> For application access

More information on authorization grant types can be found in Section 1.3 of the OAuth 2.0 RFC document.[14]

Using the Bearer Token

The *Bearer Token* is one of the most used default token types in the OAuth 2.0 standard. When the server's token endpoint retrieves a request for a new token, it recognizes the type `bearer` and provides a default Access Token according to the specification. This token is not further encrypted or signed—if this is something you are interested in, the token type `MAC` (which stands for Message Authentication Code)

---

13 *https://aaronparecki.com/2012/07/29/2/oauth2-simplified#authorization*

14 *http://tools.ietf.org/html/rfc6749#Section-1.3*

is what you're looking for.[15] An alternative to this type is utilizing JSON Web Tokens.[16]

There are three different ways to use Bearer Tokens in practice. The first option is using Request Header Fields to provide the Access Token: `Authorization: Bearer 4ae6ce68-4c59-4313-94e2-fcc2932cf5ca`.

Second, the token can be passed in the request's body as a form-encoded parameter named `access_token`. In order for this to work, the request's `Content-Type` header needs to be set to `application/x-www-form-urlencoded` and all further body parameters need to comply to the encoding requirements—JavaScript's method `encodeURI Component()` comes in handy here.

When providing the Access Token as a URI query parameter, use `access_token` followed by the Access Token itself. This last method is least desirable, because URLs might be logged. If neither using the `Authorization` header nor passing the Access Token via the request body is an option for you, make sure to send a `Cache-Control` header that is set to `no-store`. Further security considerations are being outlined in Section 5 of the official Bearer Token RFC.[17]

Authorization and Authentication with OpenID Connect

Now that we have discussed OAuth 2.0 in detail, it is time to highlight OpenID Connect. OpenID traditionally stands for an authentication framework that was widely adopted in the pre-2010 era. With the rise of OAuth and the users' wish to adopt multiple identities based on the authentication use case, a variety of hybrid extensions and so-called pseudo-authentication using OAuth became popular. OpenID Connect is a standard issued by the OpenID Foundation (*http://openid.net/foundation*) in February 2014 and resembles an extra layer on top of the OAuth 2.0 core that handles user authentication in a standardized REST-like manner.[18] All data being transmitted is formatted using JSON. While OAuth is supposed to be a standard for authorization, OpenID Connect enables authentication use cases leveraging the OAuth 2.0 protocol. This pretty much means that OpenID Connect is a superset of OAuth 2.0.

UserInfo endpoint and Claims

Next to OAuth's authorization and token endpoint, OpenID Connect relies on an additional endpoint called *UserInfo*. This endpoint provides *Claims* about the authen-

---

15 *https://tools.ietf.org/html/draft-ietf-oauth-v2-http-mac-05*

16 *http://tools.ietf.org/html/rfc7519*

17 *https://tools.ietf.org/html/rfc6750#Section-5*

18 *http://openid.net/2014/02/26/the-openid-foundation-launches-the-openid-connect-standard*

ticated user. Claims are a predefined set of profile information about the user such as the user's name, the profile's URL, or whether the user's email address has been verified.[19] Additionally, an Address Claim can be requested and custom Claims can be defined.

User authentication

OpenID Connect enables handling a user's login or determining whether a user is logged in already.

The ID Token

A central part of the OpenID Connect specification is the ID Token.[20] The token's functionality revolves around the following details:

- It serves as security token.
- It contains authentication information.
- It is signed using JSON Web Signatures (JWS).[21]
- It can be encrypted using JSON Web Encryption (JWE).[22]

 At the time of writing this book, both JWS and JWE are still works in progress.

Security Considerations Between OAuth 2 and OAuth 1.0a

As highlighted in this chapter's introduction, OAuth 1.0a's security relies heavily on client-side cryptography mechanisms. Use of TLS or SSL is not enforced and important credentials like the consumer secret and token secret are stored in plain text. Phishing attacks are a possibility and require the user to verify the authenticity of websites before providing any credentials.[23]

19 *http://openid.net/specs/openid-connect-core-1_0.html#StandardClaims*

20 *http://openid.net/specs/openid-connect-core-1_0.html#IDToken*

21 *https://tools.ietf.org/html/draft-ietf-jose-json-web-signature-41*

22 *https://tools.ietf.org/html/draft-ietf-jose-json-web-encryption-40*

23 *http://oauth.net/core/1.0a/#anchor32*

OAuth 2.0, on the other hand, relies on TLS version 1.0 as a security mechanism.[24] Additionally, protection against cross-site request forgery, known as CSRF attacks, can be achieved by utilizing the `state` parameter as outlined under the Authorization Codes section of the specification.[25]

Building an OAuth 2.0 Server

This section covers an implementation of OAuth 2.0 for the Node.js web application framework *Express* (*http://expressjs.com*). Express serves as base for many web projects and is listed as one of the most popular packages hosted on npm, the Node package manager.

To allow for seamless authentication and authorization mechanisms between the server's different routes, a feature called *middleware* will be leveraged. Middleware can be used on an application level, a route level, and to handle errors. You can imagine middleware as a function that can be plugged into your application's routes and is able to interact with the request and response objects. Popular examples for third-party middleware are `cookie-parser`, which enables parsing cookie headers, and `passport`, which is a popular middleware for handling user authentication.

> Since version 4.x of Express, the only built-in middleware is `express.static`; this function is responsible for serving static assets.[26]

Creating the Express Application

Before we can get started with the OAuth 2.0 server integration, we need to take a few minutes to set up our environment. Please refer to Appendix B for instructions on installing and setting up Node.js and the Express generator accordingly.

Following the installation of the generator, we will create our first Express application:

```
express oauth
cd oauth
npm install
npm start
```

---

24 *http://tools.ietf.org/html/rfc6749#Section-1.6*

25 *https://tools.ietf.org/html/rfc6749#section-10.12*

26 *http://expressjs.com/en/guide/using-middleware.html#middleware.built-in*

This creates a new Express application in the folder *oauth* and installs the required dependencies. The command `npm start` runs our application, which will be served on `http://localhost:3000/` (unless specified otherwise).

That's all it takes to create our first Express application! We will use this knowledge in our upcoming samples throughout this book.

Setting Up Our Server's Database

To allow for interaction with MongoDB (*https://www.mongodb.org*), our project's database, we will use the database connector *mongoose.js* (*http://mongoosejs.com*). To install the package, execute `npm install mongoose --save` from the root folder of your application. The `--save` option for the `npm install` command makes sure that an entry for Mongoose is added to our project's *package.json* file as a runtime dependency. This is important because the *node_modules* folder, where all the installed modules reside, is usually not pushed to the server.

First, we need to set up the code that allows us to connect to our MongoDB database. Add the following code snippet to the *app.js* file that the Express generator created for you:

```
var mongoose = require('mongoose');
mongoose.connect('mongodb://localhost/book');
```

For development purposes, we will use a local database (obviously this would change when deploying this application onto a different environment). By connecting to Mongoose within *app.js*, we provide application-wide access to the database itself—a necessity for having the ability to handle database queries and object manipulation within our application's routes.

Generating Authorization Codes and Tokens

Two types of tokens are relevant for our OAuth 2.0 integration. A key requirement for OAuth Tokens is that they need to be unique, nonsequential, and nonguessable.

Authorization Codes

Authorization Codes are used in redirection-based authorization flows. A code can be used only once, and a maximum lifetime of 10 minutes is recommended by the official specification.[27]

A typical authorization server response contains the parameters listed in Table 4-1.

---

27 *http://tools.ietf.org/html/rfc6749#Section-4.1.2*

Table 4-1. Authorization request response

Parameter	Necessity	Description
code	Required	An access grant that is bound to the client's redirect URL and identifier
state	Required[a]	Used to prevent cross-site request forgery

[a] Providing the state parameter in the authorization response is required when it is submitted in the authorization request

Access Tokens

Access Tokens are tokens with a short lifetime that are used to access protected resources. The short lifetime is a built-in security mechanism that tries to prevent any fraudulent usage of resources. Using the Access Token to access resources consumes the token. Securing HTTP requests to access OAuth 2.0–protected resources is also known as *Bearer Token* usage. Table 4-2 contains a complete overview of an Access Token endpoint response.

Access Tokens in OAuth 1.0

An Access Token in OAuth 1.0 is valid until it is revoked manually.

Table 4-2. Defining a successful Access Token response

Parameter	Necessity	Description
access_token	Required	The Access Token issued by the authorization server
token_type	Required	Helps the client utilize the Access Token with resource requests
expires_in	Recommended	Lifetime in seconds
scope	Optional	The scope of resources that can be accessed
refresh_token	Optional	Used to refresh the Access Token with the same authorization grant

Refresh Tokens

Refresh Tokens allow refreshing Access Tokens after they are consumed or expired. In order to allow for refreshing the Access Tokens, Refresh Tokens are long-lived and expire after they have been used to refresh the Access Token. This feature can also be used to request Access Tokens with a narrower scope, and its implementation is optional.

Generation of codes and tokens

To ensure complete uniqueness of tokens and authorization codes, various packages for Node.js can be leveraged in order to generate UUIDs. Two of the popular modules to generate UUIDs are *hat* (*http://github.com/substack/node-hat*) and *node-uuid* (*http://github.com/broofa/node-uuid*).

In order to use hat, we will use npm:

```
npm install hat --save
```

After the module is installed and the entry added to our *package.json* file, we can start working with hat to create UUIDs:

```
var hat = require('hat');
var token = hat();
```

To avoid collisions, the function rack() can be used:

```
var hat = require('hat');
var rack = hat.rack();
var token = rack();
```

node-uuid, another solution to generate UUIDs, can be installed using npm, too:

```
npm install node-uuid --save
```

Next, we obtain access to the module and generate UUIDs using the v4 method:

```
var uuid = require('node-uuid');
var token = uuid.v4(); // Unique token
```

Both hat and node-uuid allow for passing additional parameters to further randomize the generated tokens. Please refer to the individual documentation for more details. For any further examples in this book, we will stick with using node-uuid. Both modules can be exchanged mutually based on your own preference.

If we were to generate a unique string using a self-implemented method, we might consider JavaScript's Math.random() as a feasible choice to build upon. Considering its pseudorandom nature a different method like hat or node-uuid should be used, though.[28] Adam Hyland published a fantastic article on the nature of Math.random() in 2013—you should definitely read it when considering the use of this method.[29]

Official Documentation of Math.random() from ES5

Returns a Number value with positive sign, greater than or equal to 0 but less than 1, chosen randomly or pseudo randomly with approximately uniform distribution over that range, using an implementation-dependent algorithm or strategy. This function takes no arguments.

---

28 See the documentation here, *http://es5.github.io/x15.8.html#x15.8.2.14*

29 *https://bocoup.com/weblog/random-numbers*

The correct implementation if UUIDs requires three criteria:

- They must be universally unique.
- They must be nonsequential.
- They must be nonguessable.

Using a database's identifier like MongoDB's `ObjectId` is not recommended because we cannot guarantee the preceding requirements will be met. `ObjectId` is a 12-byte BSON type and consists of the following elements:[30]

- A 4-byte value representing the seconds since the Unix epoch
- A 3-byte machine identifier
- A 2-byte process ID
- A 3-byte counter, starting with a random value

The Authorization Endpoint

As discussed in the introductory section for OAuth 2.0, the Authorization Code flow requires two endpoints to be implemented in order to work. First, we will look at implementing the authorization endpoint:

```
var uuid = require('node-uuid');
var Client = require('../lib/models/client');
var AuthCode = require('../lib/models/authcode');

router.get('/authorize', function(req, res, next) {
  var responseType = req.query.response_type;
  var clientId = req.query.client_id;
  var redirectUri = req.query.redirect_uri;
  var scope = req.query.scope;
  var state = req.query.state;

  if (!responseType) {
    // cancel the request - we miss the response type
  }

  if (responseType !== 'code') {
    // notify the user about an unsupported response type
  }

  if (!clientId) {
    // cancel the request - client id is missing
  }
```

---

30 See the documentation here, *http://docs.mongodb.org/manual/reference/object-id*

```
Client.findOne({
  clientId: clientId
}, function (err, client) {
  if (err) {
    // handle the error by passing it to the middleware
    next(err);
  }

  if (!client) {
    // cancel the request - the client does not exist
  }

  if (redirectUri !== client.redirectUri) {
    // cancel the request
  }

  if (scope !== client.scope) {
    // handle the scope
  }

  var authCode = new AuthCode({
    clientId: clientId,
    userId: client.userId,
    redirectUri: redirectUri
  });
  authCode.save();

  var response = {
    state: state,
    code: authCode.code
  };

  if (redirectUri) {
    var redirect = redirectUri +
      '?code=' + response.code +
      (state === undefined ? '' : '&state=' + state);
    res.redirect(redirect);
  } else {
    res.json(response);
  }
});
});
```

The preceding code assumes that there is a Mongoose model called `Client`. A client consists of an ID, a secret, a user ID, and a few other attributes like the redirect URI it uses in order to communicate with the Consumer.

When the redirect client flow is being used, the code is provided as query parameter —in case of a resource request, a JSON object containing both the state and the code is returned.

One of the attributes of a client is also the scope. The scope tells the Service Provider which kind of attributes the Consumer is allowed to access. When obtaining the user's authorization, clients usually display the scopes in order to make sure that users understand what kind of information they share.

Our application requires client credentials to be passed in both the /authorization and /token routes. Client IDs, secrets, and names are required to be unique in order to avoid any issues. We will build upon MongoDB's schema mechanisms to realize this challenge. One mechanism is that properties can be flagged as unique in order to avoid duplicate keys in the database:

```
var mongoose = require('mongoose');
var uuid = require('node-uuid');

var ClientModel = function() {
  var clientSchema = mongoose.Schema({
    clientId:     { type: String, default: uuid.v4(), unique: true },
    clientSecret: { type: String, default: uuid.v4(), unique: true },
    createdAt:    { type: Date,   default: Date.now },
    name:         { type: String, unique: true },
    scope:        { type: String },
    userId:       { type: String },
    redirectUri:  { type: String }
  });

  return mongoose.model('Client', clientSchema);
};

module.exports = new ClientModel();
```

In ClientModel we use MongoDB's default initialization to our advantage. Instead of having to pass a client ID and secret whenever we create a client, this process is shifted to the database schema itself.

When dealing with attributes that are flagged as unique—such as the client's name—we need to check whether the database entry was created successfully. When using the save() method, you'll notice that mongoose and the underlying MongoDB won't provide feedback on whether the operation was successful. This is where a callback mechanism can be used. By checking whether an error occurred before rendering the client's details, we can ensure that we avoid confusion and problems:

```
router.get('/', function(req, res, next) {
  var client = new Client({
    name: 'Test',
    userId: 1,
    redirectUri: 'http://localhost:5000/callback'
  });
  client.save(function(err) {
    if (err) {
      next(new Error('Client name exists already'));
```

```
      } else {
        res.json(client);
      }
    });
  });
```

When implementing this route, you'll want to pair it with a form that allows users to enter a client name, select scopes (which will be required for OpenID Connect), and the client's redirect URI.

AuthCode, another Mongoose model we rely on, is implemented in a similar manner. It represents the authorization codes our application issues in /authorize:

```
var mongoose = require('mongoose');
var uuid = require('node-uuid');

var AuthCodeModel = function() {
  var authCodeSchema = mongoose.Schema({
    code:        { type: String,  default: uuid.v4() },
    createdAt:   { type: Date,    default: Date.now, expires: '10m' },
    consumed:    { type: Boolean, default: false },
    clientId:    { type: String },
    userId:      { type: String },
    redirectUri: { type: String }
  });

  return mongoose.model('AuthCode', authCodeSchema);
};

module.exports = new AuthCodeModel();
```

Handling a Token's Lifetime

In this example, we will look at creating and storing tokens using *mongoose.js*, handling the token's lifetime, and consuming the token afterward. For our application, we will use a Token TTL of 3 minutes.

First we will set up a new Mongoose schema[31] called Token. The schema will consist of the details outlined in the OAuth 2.0 specification:

```
var mongoose = require('mongoose');
var uuid = require('node-uuid');

var TokenModel = function() {
  var tokenSchema = mongoose.Schema({
    userId:       { type: String },
    refreshToken: { type: String,  unique: true },
    accessToken:  { type: String,  default: uuid.v4() },
```

---

31 *http://mongoosejs.com/docs/guide.html*

```
  expiresIn:   { type: String,   default: '10800' },
  tokenType:   { type: String,   default: 'bearer' },
  consumed:    { type: Boolean,  default: false },
  createdAt:   { type: Date,     default: Date.now,  expires: '3m' }
});

  return mongoose.model('Token', tokenSchema);
};

module.exports = new TokenModel();
```

You will notice that an expires flag has been defined. It's set to 3 minutes and will cause the database entry to be deleted (other values like 1h or simple integers for seconds can be used here too). In order to make creating Access Tokens as easy as writing a few lines of code, sensible default values for fields like tokenType are being used.

The Access Token is initialized using the node-uuid module in order to populate the accessToken and refreshToken fields. userId identifies the resource owner and can be used to consume all Access Tokens that were assigned to the user.

By providing the user's ID to both the RefreshToken and Token objects, we can ensure that we are able to consume all issued tokens at once:

```
var mongoose = require('mongoose');
var uuid = require('node-uuid');

var RefreshTokenModel = function() {
  var refreshTokenSchema = mongoose.Schema({
    userId:     { type: String },
    token:      { type: String,   default: uuid.v4() },
    createdAt:  { type: Date,     default: Date.now },
    consumed:   { type: Boolean,  default: false }
  });

  return mongoose.model('RefreshToken', refreshTokenSchema);
};

module.exports = new RefreshTokenModel();
```

After defining the Access Token and Refresh Token schema, we're able to generate both of them like this:

```
var uuid = require('node-uuid');
var Token = require('../lib/models/token');
var RefreshToken = require('../lib/models/refreshtoken');

var userId = 1; // some id

var refreshToken = new RefreshToken({
  userId: userId
});
refreshToken.save();
```

```
var token = new Token({
  refreshToken: refreshToken.token,
  userId: userId
});
token.save();
```

If we put all of this together, we can begin implementing our token endpoint. For the first implementation of this route, we will refrain from handling Refresh Tokens that were obtained before—we cover handling them in "Using Refresh Tokens" on page 81 after covering some more basics. Here's the code for our first draft:

```
var AuthCode = require('../lib/models/authcode');
var Client = require('../lib/models/client');
var Token = require('../lib/models/token');
var RefreshToken = require('../lib/models/refreshtoken');

router.post('/token', function (req, res) {
  var grantType = req.body.grant_type;
  var authCode = req.body.code;
  var redirectUri = req.body.redirect_uri;
  var clientId = req.body.client_id;

  if (!grantType) {
    // no grant type passed - cancel this request
  }

  if (grantType === 'authorization_code') {
    AuthCode.findOne({
      code: authCode
    }, function(err, code) {
      if (err) {
        // handle the error
      }

      if (!code) {
        // no valid authorization code provided - cancel
      }

      if (code.consumed) {
        // the code got consumed already - cancel
      }

      code.consumed = true;
      code.save();

      if (code.redirectUri !== redirectUri) {
        // cancel the request
      }

      // validate the client id - an extra security measure
      Client.findOne({
```

```
      clientId: clientId
    }, function(error, client) {
      if (error) {
        // the client id provided was a mismatch or does not exist
      }

      if (!client) {
        // the client id provided was a mismatch or does not exist
      }

      var _refreshToken = new RefreshToken({
        userId: code.userId
      });
      _refreshToken.save();

      var _token = new Token({
        refreshToken: _refreshToken.token,
        userId: code.userId
      });
      _token.save();

      // send the new token to the consumer
      var response = {
        access_token: _token.accessToken,
        refresh_token: _token.refreshToken,
        expires_in: _token.expiresIn,
        token_type: _token.tokenType
      };

      res.json(response);
    });
  });
  }
});
```

Now our server is ready to issue Access Tokens in order to allow the Consumer to access protected resources.

Handling Resource Requests

Whenever a resource is accessed using the Access Token, the token needs to be consumed in order to make sure no more resource requests are made using this token:

```
var Token = require('../lib/models/token');
var accessToken = 'some uuid';

Token.findOne({
  accessToken: accessToken
}, function(err, token) {
  if (err) {
    // handle the error
  }
```

```
    if (!token) {
      // no token found - cancel
    }

    if (token.consumed) {
      // the token got consumed already - cancel
    }

    // consume all tokens - including the one used
    Token.update({
      userId: token.userId,
      consumed: false
    }, {
      $set: { consumed: true }
    });
  });
```

Mongoose's findOne and update functions are practical when dealing with tokens because we can easily consume all tokens for a certain user or check whether a token is still valid.

This method makes for convenient middleware that protects our application's resources. Let's apply this to an Express route:

```
var Token = require('../models/token');

var authorize = function(req, res, next) {
  var accessToken;

  // check the authorization header
  if (req.headers.authorization) {
    // validate the authorization header
    var parts = req.headers.authorization.split(' ');

    if (parts.length < 2) {
      // no access token got provided - cancel
      res.set('WWW-Authenticate', 'Bearer');
      res.sendStatus('401');
      return;
    }

    accessToken = parts[1];
  } else {
    // access token URI query parameter or entity body
    accessToken = req.query.access_token || req.body.access_token;
  }

  if (!accessToken) {
    // no access token got provided - cancel with a 401
  }
```

```
Token.findOne({
  accessToken: accessToken
}, function(err, token) {
  // Same as in above example
  ...

  // consume all tokens - including the one used
  Token.update({
    userId: token.userId,
    consumed: false
  }, {
    $set: { consumed: true }
  });

  // ready to access protected resources
  next();
  });
};

module.exports = authorize;
```

After the authorization middleware has processed the request, the request is passed on to the next middleware or the route itself by executing `next()`.

Authorizing requests using the authorization middleware we just implemented is as easy as adding it to our resources route:

```
var express = require('express');
var router = express.Router();
var authorize = require('../lib/middleware/authorize');

router.get('/user', authorize, function (req, res) {
  var user = {
    name: 'Tim Messerschmidt',
    country: 'Germany'
  }
  res.json(user);
});

module.exports = router;
```

Additional middleware can be passed by using array-syntax instead. If we were to use another middleware that logs all requests, the /user definition would change to the following:

```
router.get('/user', [logger, authorize], function (req, res) {
  var user = {
    name: 'Tim Messerschmidt',
    country: 'Germany'
  }
  res.json(user);
});
```

Using Refresh Tokens

The Refresh Token is being used to obtain a new Access Token. In order to do so, the Consumer communicates with the Service Provider's token endpoint. In the next example, we will continue working on the token endpoint we have implemented in order to issue Access Tokens in exchange for Authorization Codes.

The key difference for this scenario is the different Grant Type `refresh_token`; it indicates that the client obtained an Access Token before and is now trying to obtain new credentials in order to continue accessing protected resources:

```
var AuthCode = require('../lib/models/authcode');
var Token = require('../lib/models/token');
var RefreshToken = require('../lib/models/refreshtoken');

router.post('/token', function(req, res) {
  var grantType = req.body.grant_type;
  var refreshToken = req.body.refresh_token;
  var authCode = req.body.code;
  var redirectUri = req.body.redirect_uri;
  var clientId = req.body.client_id;

  if (!grantType) {
    // no grant type provided - cancel
  }

  if (grantType === 'authorization_code') {
    ...
  } else if (grantType === 'refresh_token') {
    if (!refreshToken) {
      // no refresh token provided - cancel
    }

    RefreshToken.findOne({
      token: refreshToken
    }, function (err, token) {
      if (err) {
        // handle the error
      }

      if (!token) {
        // no refresh token found
      }

      if (token.consumed) {
        // the token got consumed already
      }

      // consume all previous refresh tokens
      RefreshToken.update({
        userId: token.userId,
```

```
      consumed: false
    }, {
      $set: {consumed: true}
    });

    var _refreshToken = new RefreshToken({
      userId: token.userId
    });
    _refreshToken.save();

    var _token = new Token({
      refreshToken: _refreshToken.token,
      userId: token.userId
    });
    _token.save();

    var response = {
      access_token: _token.accessToken,
      refresh_token: _token.refreshToken,
      expires_in: _token.expiresIn,
      token_type: _token.tokenType
    };

    // send the new token to the consumer
    res.json(response);
    });
  }
});
```

You will notice that using the token endpoint with Refresh Tokens is very similar to the code we have used before to authorize requests using Access Tokens. After applying some basic parameter checks, the tokens are being consumed using the update-mechanism, and the next action—in this case, issuing a new Access Token—is executed.

Handling Errors

In this section's code listings, we've mostly looked at success cases and covered error-handling through comments. This subsection covers how to handle errors according to the OAuth spec utilizing Express's response object.

Before we dive into OAuth's specification again, a quick look into HTTP status[32] codes reveals that there is a selection of codes (Table 4-3) that will be interesting for us.

---

32 *https://www.w3.org/Protocols/rfc2616/rfc2616-sec10.html*

Table 4-3. Relevant HTTP status codes

Code	Name	Description
302	Found	The user agent *must not* automatically redirect. Can be used in routes such as the Authorization Request.
400	Bad Request	Malformed request.
401	Unauthorized	Authentication failed or not provided. Response must contain `WWW-Authenticate` header.
403	Forbidden	Even though an authentication might have happened, the requesting party is not authorized to access the underlying resources.
500	Internal Server Error	An unexpected condition occurred and the server cannot handle the request.
503	Service Unavailable	The server might be overloaded and cannot handle the request at this time.

These status codes provide us with a toolkit to handle different use cases in the authentication and authorization we encounter throughout the OAuth flow. OAuth's specification provides error codes that need to be provided in order to help the implementer identify potential sources of errors[33] (Table 4-4).

Table 4-4. OAuth error codes

Code	Description
`invalid_request`	Parameters missing, invalid parameter value provided, or parameters might be duplicates.
`unauthorized_client`	Malformed request.
`access_denied`	The resource owner or authorization server denied the request.
`unsupported_response_type`	The authorization server does not support obtaining an authorization code using this method.
`invalid_scope`	The requested scope is invalid, unknown, or malformed.
`invalid_grant`	The provided authorization grant or Refresh Token is invalid, expired, or the client details don't match those defined in the authorization request (redirect URI, different client).
`server_error`	Internal server error that can be used when a 500 error cannot be returned to the client.
`temporarily_unavailable`	The server is currently unable to handle the request. Can be used in redirect scenarios where a 503 cannot be returned.

Please note that these error codes differ based on the current step in the authentication flow.

---

[33] *http://tools.ietf.org/html/rfc6749#section-4.1.1*

Using the knowledge we've acquired about the tools that both HTTP/1.1 and OAuth 2.0 provide, we can advance to building our own error-handling class:

```
var util = require('util');

function OAuthError(code, message, err) {
  Error.call(this);
  Error.captureStackTrace(this, this.constructor);

  if (err instanceof Error) {
    this.stack = err.stack;
    this.message = message || err.message;
  } else {
    this.message = message || '';
  }
  this.code = code;

  switch (code) {
    case 'unsupported_grant_type':
      this.status = 400;
      break;
    case 'invalid_grant':
      this.status = 400;
      break;
    case 'invalid_request':
      this.status = 400;
      break;
    case 'invalid_client':
      this.status = 401;
      break;
    case 'invalid_token':
      this.status = 401;
      break;
    case 'server_error':
      this.status = 503;
      break;
    default:
      // Leave all other errors to the default error handler
      this.status = 500;
      break;
  }

  return this;
}

util.inherits(OAuthError, Error);

module.exports = OAuthError;
```

Because OAuthError is an extension of Error and is supposed to be used toward Express's error-handling mechanism (via using next or throwing an error), Node's util module is used in order to inherit all Error methods and properties. The OAuth specification allows us to define custom error codes (such as `invalid_token`) to refine the interaction with clients.

Because the routes handling `POST` requests don't have access to the `next` parameter, we set up a new handler:

```
function handleError(err, res) {
  res.set('Cache-Control', 'no-store');
  res.set('Pragma', 'no-cache');

  if (err.code === 'invalid_client') {
    var header = 'Bearer realm="book", error="invalid_token",' +
      'error_description="No access token provided"';
    res.set('WWW-Authenticate', header);
  }
  res.status(err.status).send({
    error: err.code,
    description: err.message
  });
}

module.exports = handleError;
```

The default behavior is to turn off caching by providing both the `Cache-Control` and `Pragma` (nowadays mostly obsolete) headers to the client. This ensures the freshness of information provided.

Using error handlers

After we've extended the `Error` class to be able to provide more meaningful feedback to the client, we can implement this accordingly to handle all cases that apply to our current scenarios.

The first step is to make both the `OAuthError` class and the `handleError` function available via `require`:

```
// Require custom error handling
var OAuthError = require('../lib/errors/oautherror');
var errorHandler = require('../lib/errors/handler');
```

For `GET` requests, we can build upon middleware once more. By using the command-chain, we simply hand over the `OAuthError` to the appropriate handler—the Express generator creates one by default that renders the status code and error message (when running in a development environment):

```
// development error handler
// will print stacktrace
if (app.get('env') === 'development') {
  app.use(function(err, req, res) {
    console.log('error');
    res.status(err.status || 500);
```

```
    res.render('error', {
      message: err.message,
      error: err
    });
  });
}

// production error handler
// no stacktraces leaked to user
app.use(function(err, req, res) {
  console.log('error');
  res.status(err.status || 500);
  res.render('error', {
    message: err.message,
    error: {}
  });
});
```

When checking whether the GET request was populated according to OAuth's requirements, we can simply invoke the error handler like this:

```
if (!responseType) {
  next(new OAuthError('invalid_request',
    'Missing parameter: response_type'));
}
```

For POST requests, we alter the code slightly. In this example, we validate that the Authorization Code has been consumed before issuing a new Access Token:

```
if (code.consumed) {
  return errorHandler(new OAuthError('invalid_grant',
    'Authorization Code expired'), res);
}
```

You will notice that this time we invoke the errorHandler and pass the response object in order to set the status and error message accordingly.

Adding OpenID Connect Functionality to the Server

Now that we've discussed how to implement OAuth 2.0 on the server by adding both the /token and /authorize endpoints, this section highlights how to build upon our existing implementation by adding OpenID Connect functionality on top. Before we add the userinfo endpoint, we should examine the ID Token (Table 4-5), OpenID Connect's security mechanism of proving authentication and authorization.

Table 4-5. The basics of an ID Token[a]

Parameter	Necessity	Description
iss	Required	Issuer Identifier—comes as URL using https scheme and contains host, port, path https://example.com
sub	Required	Subject Identifier—*must not* exceed 255 ASCII characters
aud	Required	The ID Token's audience—*must* contain the OAuth client_id
exp	Required	Expiration time
iat	Required	Time at which the token was issued
nonce	Required*	If present the nonce must be verified
auth_time	Optional	Time at which the user authentication occurred
acr	Optional	Authentication Context Class Reference
amr	Optional	Authentication Methods References
azp	Optional	Authorized party—*must* contain the OAuth client_id

[a] *http://openid.net/specs/openid-connect-core-1_0.html#IDToken*

OpenID Connect tokens are JSON Web Tokens that must be signed using JWS and can then be optionally signed and encrypted using JWS and JWE. One popular module choice to handle JWT with Node is njwt, which handles signing tokens via HS256 per default.[34]

The ID Token Schema

As with the other tokens that we've been using in this example so far, we will create a new Mongoose schema that will handle the generation and expiry of our ID Token:

```
var mongoose = require('mongoose');
var uuid = require('node-uuid');

var IdTokenModel = function() {
  var idTokenSchema = mongoose.Schema({
    createdAt: { type: Date,   default: Date.now, expires: '1m' },
    iat:       { type: String, default: Math.floor(new Date() / 1000) },
    exp:       { type: String, default: Math.floor(new Date() / 1000) + 180 },
    sub:       { type: String, default: uuid.v4(), maxlength: 255 },
    iss:       { type: String },
    aud:       { type: String },
    userId:    { type: String }
  });

  return mongoose.model('IdToken', idTokenSchema);
```

---

34 *https://www.npmjs.com/package/njwt*

```
};

module.exports = new IdTokenModel();
```

The ID Token specification requires the `iat` and `exp` values to represent the seconds since 1970-01-01T0:0:0Z UTC.[35] We achieve this by using JavaScript's `Date` class, which returns the milliseconds since Unix Epoch and get the seconds by dividing the result by 1,000.[36] `Math.floor` rounds down the result to the next integer.

Modifying the Authorization Endpoint

When dealing with a regular OAuth 2 authorization flow, the `scope` parameter is considered optional and serves the purpose of defining resources that will be accessed on top of handling a simple login with OAuth. This behavior changes when we decide to use OpenID Connect as our Authorization and Authentication framework, though. OpenID Connect's specification defines multiple scope values that can be passed in order to specify which pieces of profile information are required by the client. The minimum scope that needs to be passed is `openid`; this tells the server that an OpenID Connect authorization attempt is being made.

Considering the required scope as just outlined, we will go ahead and modify the authorization endpoint accordingly:

```
router.get('/authorize', function(req, res, next) {
  var responseType = req.query.response_type;
  var clientId = req.query.client_id;
  var redirectUri = req.query.redirect_uri;
  var scope = req.query.scope;
  var state = req.query.state;
  var userId = req.query.user_id;

  // Same as in above example
  ...

  if (!scope || scope.indexOf('openid') < 0) {
      next(new OAuthError('invalid_scope',
        'Scope is missing or not well-defined'));
  }

  Client.findOne({
    clientId: clientId
  }, function (err, client) {
    ...

    if (scope !== client.scope) {
```

---

35 *http://openid.net/specs/openid-connect-core-1_0.html#IDToken*

36 *https://developer.mozilla.org/en-US/docs/Web/JavaScript/Reference/Global_Objects/Date*

```
      next(new OAuthError('invalid_scope',
        'Scope is missing or not well-defined'));
    }

    ...
  });
});
```

In this example, we have made the basic assumption that each request to the endpoint is an OpenID Connect authentication request. Another way of handling the request is handling all requests with a scope containing openid as OpenID Connect, and all other requests as OAuth 2.

Instead of checking the scope parameter in the initial statements, we move the conditional statement down to the Client section and will check if we are dealing with an OpenID Connect authentication request. The OpenID Connect specification does not specify how to handle non-openid scope requests—the fallback to OAuth 2 seems to be a sensible choice, though:

```
if (scope && scope.indexOf('openid') >= 0) {
  // OpenID Connect Authentication request - generate an ID Token
}
```

Adjusting the Token Endpoint

While the changes to the authorization endpoint are minimal and easy to handle, we need to make a few more changes to our token endpoint. The client's request will practically stay the same, but we'll need to create the ID Token, store that token, and pass it to the client with our Access Token response.

One of the new requirements for the token endpoint is verifying if the Grant Type (the Authorization Code we pass to the token endpoint) is the result of an OpenID Connect authentication request—otherwise, the endpoint is not supposed to return an ID Token:

```
router.post('/token', function (req, res) {
  var grantType = req.body.grant_type;
  var refreshToken = req.body.refresh_token;
  var authCode = req.body.code;
  var redirectUri = req.body.redirect_uri;
  var clientId = req.body.client_id;

  if (!grantType) {
    return errorHandler(
      new OAuthError('invalid_request',
      'Missing parameter: grant_type'),
      res);
  }

  if (grantType === 'authorization_code') {
```

```
AuthCode.findOne({
  code: authCode
}, function (err, code) {
  // the same validation as for the OAuth 2 flow
  ...

  Client.findOne({
    clientId: clientId
  }, function (error, client) {
    // same as in the OAuth 2 example
    ...

    var _token;
    var response;
    if (client.scope && (client.scope.indexOf('openid') >= 0)) {
      // An OpenID Connect request
      var _idToken = new IdToken({
        iss: client.redirectUri,
        aud: client.clientId,
        userId: code.userId
      });
      _idToken.save();

      _token = new Token({
        refreshToken: _refreshToken.token,
        idToken: _idToken.sub,
        userId: code.userId
      });
      _token.save();

      // send the token to the consumer
      response = {
        access_token: _token.accessToken,
        refresh_token: _token.refreshToken,
        id_token: _idToken.sub,
        expires_in: _token.expiresIn,
        token_type: _token.tokenType
      };

      res.json(response);
    } else {
      // An OAuth 2 request
      _token = new Token({
        refreshToken: _refreshToken.token,
        userId: code.userId
      });
      _token.save();

      // send the token to the consumer
      response = {
        access_token: _token.accessToken,
        refresh_token: _token.refreshToken,
```

```
                expires_in: _token.expiresIn,
                token_type: _token.tokenType
            };

            res.json(response);
          }
        });
      });
    });
  });
```

The UserInfo Endpoint

After we have adjusted the authentication and token endpoints, the last adjustment we need to handle is adding a new endpoint called UserInfo. The UserInfo endpoint shares the resource owner's profile information with the client. All requests to this endpoint must be signed using the OAuth 2 Access Token provided as the Authorization header.

Because we have already written the middleware that handles OAuth 2–based authorization, adding the UserInfo endpoint is as easy as adding this new route:

```
router.get('/userinfo', authorize, function(req, res) {
  // The request got authorized - share profile information
  ...
});
```

This example outlines the power of middleware. Instead of writing duplicate code to handle simple tasks like checking the Authorization header, we simply mount a middleware that handles this task for all relevant routes.

Session Management with OpenID Connect

OpenID Connect Session Management is a draft that proposes the ability to control end-user sessions to the OpenID Connect stack.[37] This would enable the functionality to not just log in the user (as a lot of OAuth 2 clients do) but also handle the termination of sessions—the actual logout process.

The specification proposes to pass three parameters to the Service Provider in order to allow for logging out the user. id_token_hint is a required parameter that matches the previously issued ID Token and identifies the authenticated end-user plus the user's session. The parameter post_logout_redirect_uri will be used for redirects after the logout and is optional. Finally, the parameter state can be passed as an additional security mechanism; after the logout, it will be passed on to the post_log out_redirect_uri as a query parameter. state is an optional parameter, too.

---

37 *https://openid.net/specs/openid-connect-session-1_0.html*

Building an OAuth 2 Client

Client-side OAuth 2.0 varies based on our client's use case and flow. In the following sections, we discuss the redirection-based Authorization Code flow and how to use the credentials-based flow.

Using Authorization Codes

Authorization Codes are one of the most common OAuth 2.0 grant types. They find their usage in multiple web and mobile applications that leverage redirects in order to exchange the necessary information.

In this example, we implement another Express server that will act as the Consumer. The sample will leverage Jade, a Node template engine, and show a simple button that allows us to authorize the user.

The first step is enabling session support for Express. To do so, execute `npm install express-session --save` to install the required node module and add the following lines to your *app.js* or *index.js* file that handles the Express initialization:

```
var session = require('express-session');

app.use(session({
  secret: 'your session secret',
  resave: false,
  saveUninitialized: false,
  cookie: { maxAge: 60000 }
}));
```

The `resave` option ensures that sessions are saved even if they didn't get modified. `saveUninitialized` doesn't save new sessions before they are modified—especially when dealing with authentication and authorization purposes, it is recommended to disable this option (the default value is `true` according to the documentation[38]):

```
var express = require('express');
var router = express.Router();
var uuid = require('node-uuid');

var SEVER_URL = 'YOUR SERVER URL';
var REDIRECT_SERVER_URL = 'REDIRECT URL';

var CLIENT_ID = 'YOUR_CLIENT_ID';

router.get('/', function(req, res) {
  var state = uuid.v4();
  req.session.state = state;
```

---

[38] *https://github.com/expressjs/session#saveuninitialized*

```
var options = {
  url: SERVER_URL + '/authorize',
  client_id: CLIENT_ID,
  redirect_uri: REDIRECT_SERVER_URL + '/callback',
  state: state,
  response_type: 'code',
  user_id: 1
};

var authorizationURL = options.url +
  '?redirect_uri=' + options.redirect_uri +
  '&user_id=' + options.user_id +
  '&client_id=' + options.client_id +
  '&response_type=' + options.response_type +
  '&state=' + options.state;

res.render('index', {
  authorizationURL: authorizationURL
});
});
```

Our Express route renders a template called index and provides the authorizatio
nURL to the template in order to avoid hardcoding the Client's details into the template itself:

```
extends layout

block content
  h1 OAuth 2 Client
  a(href="#{authorizationURL}")
    button Authorize
```

After the Service Provider authorizes our client, it redirects to the specified redi
rect_uri and provides the state query parameter (if sent to the server in the previous request) and the Authorization Code itself as code.

We leverage request—a module that eases making HTTP requests—in order to request the Access Token. Install request by executing npm install request --
save:

```
var express = require('express');
var router = express.Router();

var request = require('request');

router.get('/callback', function(req, res, next) {
  var state = req.query.state;
  var code = req.query.code;

  // Compare the state with the session's state
  if (state !== req.session.state) {
```

```
      next(new Error('State does not match'));
  }

  request.post({
    url: SEVER_URL + '/token',
    form: {
      code: code,
      grant_type: 'authorization_code',
      redirect_uri: REDIRECT_SERVER_URL + '/callback',
      client_id: CLIENT_ID
    }}, function(error, response, body) {
    if (error) {
      // handle the error
      next(error);
    }

    var resp = JSON.parse(body);
    var accessToken = resp.access_token;

    // Use the Access Token for a protected resource request
    ...
  });
});
```

Node is able to perform HTTP requests without leveraging the help of any third-party modules. We chose `request` over implementing requests manually with the `http` module for simplicity and better readability.

Storing tokens on the Client

There is a big discussion about finding the most secure and most conveniently accessible storage for tokens. Realistically, an Access Token expires after a few minutes, so we can take that lifetime into consideration. For the Refresh Token, on the other hand, we deal with a far longer lifecycle and have to handle the token appropriately. From a security standpoint, we want to ensure that our tokens are not vulnerable to XSS (cross-site scripting), which means that they shouldn't be accessible from JavaScript (injections) that runs on our client. This reasoning would rule out utilizing HTML5 Web Storage. HTML5 Web Storage offers both local storage that can be accessed via `window.localStorage` and doesn't expire, and `window.sessionStorage`, a session-based storage mechanism that gets wiped as soon as the user closes the browser's tab.

Classic cookies can be flagged with the `HttpOnly` option, which ensures that the cookie's value can be accessed only from the server side. This serves as a protection mechanism against XSS attacks and leaves XSRF/CSRF attacks for discussion—a big risk that often is not accounted for. Gladly, modern web frameworks often offer security mechanisms (Which might have to be enabled in their configuration) in order to handle the threat of replay attacks and more. We discuss these concepts in depth in Chapter 6.

Custom schemes

On mobile platforms, it has become quite popular to use a custom URL scheme in order to make server-to-application calls. A URL can be broken into the following components: `scheme://host/path?query`. This allows apps to define callbacks from the Web like `myoauthapp://book/auth?callback`.

Authorization Using Resource Owner Credentials or Client Credentials

Next to the Authorization Code Grant Flow, another popular OAuth 2.0 Grant is known as the *Resource Owner Password Credentials Grant* (*https://tools.ietf.org/html/rfc6749#section-4.3*), as defined in section 4.3 of the OAuth 2.0 specification. This flow, illustrated in Figure 4-3, represents a simplified way to obtain an Access Token and involves fewer steps in doing so.

The specification describes this flow as viable for scenarios in which the user deeply trusts the client—this could be a device's operating system or a highly privileged application.

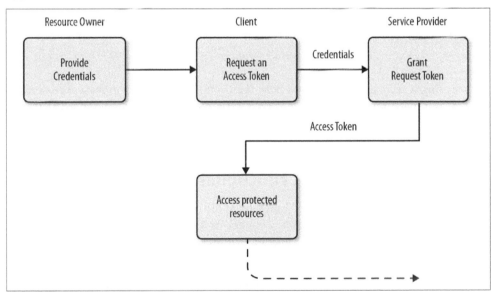

Figure 4-3. OAuth 2.0 Resource Owner Credentials Grant

The Resource Owner Credentials Grant Type (Figure 4-4) is similar to the Client Credentials Grant Type, in which the Client provides its credentials to the Service Provider. The difference is that in the first case the user trusts the client and therefore submits his details, whereas in the latter example the client owns the resources himself and therefore another step in the authentication scenario can be removed.

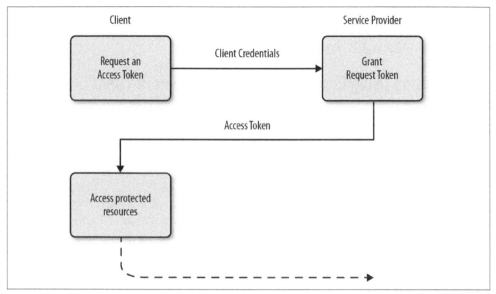

Figure 4-4. OAuth 2.0 Client Credentials Grant

As you might have guessed, in this flow the client simply asks for the user's credentials. A popular example for a Client Credentials–driven API is PayPal's REST API, which uses client credentials in order to authorize a merchant's application to accept payments.[39]

Adding OpenID Connect Functionality to the Client

Because OpenID Connect heavily relies on OAuth 2.0 in terms of communication and security mechanisms, only a few changes or additions to our client-side OAuth 2.0 example are needed in order to add support for OpenID Connect.

OpenID Connect provides two ways to handle the consumer and service provider communication. The first flow is known as *Basic Client* and is detailed in the Basic Client Implementer's Guide.[40] The second flow, the *Implicit Client*, is detailed in the

---

39 *https://developer.paypal.com/docs/api/#authentication—headers*

40 *http://openid.net/specs/openid-connect-basic-1_0.html*

Implicit Client Implementer's Guide.[41] The implicit flow is known as *client-side flow* or *implicit grant flow* and removes the need for an authorization token; the Access Token is simply sent back to the server and no Refresh Token is issued. This flow is generally seen as less secure than the basic flow and will therefore not be outlined in detail. A great post covering the OAuth 2.0 implicit flow has been written by Sven Haiges.[42]

The OpenID Connect Basic Flow

When dealing with OpenID Connect's Basic flow, we'll need to adjust the client-side OAuth 2.0 requests for authentication and accessing resources. For OAuth 2.0, the scope parameter is optional and needs to be used when added to the initial authentication request. When adding OpenID Connect functionality to the client, scope becomes a required parameter that needs to be set to cover at least openid as a scope value.[43] Table 4-6 provides an overview of common scopes that can be used.

Table 4-6. OpenID Connect request scope values

Scope value	Necessity	Description
openid	Required	Specifies that the Client is making an OpenID Connect request
profile	Optional	Access to the User's profile Claims, such as name, family_name, and given_name
email	Optional	Access to the email and email_verified Claims
address	Optional	Access to the address Claim
phone	Optional	Access to the phone_number and phone_number_verified Claims
offline_access	Optional	Request that an OAuth 2.0 Refresh Token is issued in order to allow for obtaining a new Access Token and therefore allowing to access the UserInfo endpoint even when the user is not present

The request to handle the client's authentication will be altered to this form:

```
var options = {
  url: SERVER_URL + '/authorize',
  client_id: CLIENT_ID,
  redirect_uri: REDIRECT_SERVER_URL + '/callback',
  state: state,
  scope: 'openid',
  response_type: 'code',
  user_id: 1
};
```

---

41 *http://openid.net/specs/openid-connect-implicit-1_0.html*

42 *https://labs.hybris.com/2012/06/05/oauth2-the-implicit-flow-aka-as-the-client-side-flow*

43 *http://openid.net/specs/openid-connect-basic-1_0.html#RequestParameters*

```
var authorizationURL = options.url +
  '?redirect_uri=' + options.redirect_uri +
  '&user_id=' + options.user_id +
  '&client_id=' + options.client_id +
  '&scope=' + options.scope +
  '&response_type=' + options.response_type +
  '&state=' + options.state;

res.render('index', {
  authorizationURL: authorizationURL
});
```

The difference compared to the OAuth 2 client is that this time we are required to pass the scope parameter (set to at least openid) in order to match the specifcation's minimum requirements.

After obtaining the user's authorization, the authorization code is issued and exchanged for the actual token. The token endpoint's response will differ slightly and will also contain an id_token attribute:

```
{
  "access_token": "71518132-d27b-4828-9317-5571a46c89fb",
  "refresh_token": "3ae3e757-7c32-492d-8af5-8dba943d2ec3",
  "id_token": "ee0b16a5-5be7-4629-8d1b-bf3fd7ea64a9",
  "expires_in": "10800",
  "token_type": "bearer"
}
```

The ID Token can be used as an additional security mechanism. It contains claims about the authentication of an end user as defined in the OpenID Connect specification.[44] An example value that can be easily validated is azp (authorized party) that must match the Consumer's client_id.

The OpenID Connect specification provides a list of all 21 standard Claims that can be returned by the server's UserInfo endpoint.[45] Claims must be returned in JSON format unless the format was defined differently during the client's registration.[46]

Beyond OAuth 2.0 and OpenID Connect

In this chapter, we have discussed the ins and outs of both OAuth 2.0 and OpenID Connect. Both protocols find strong adoption within the industry and empower millions of users and a multitude of applications. Still, with the rise of mobile apps and especially mobile authentication and authorization, the need to provide a better user

---

44 *http://openid.net/specs/openid-connect-core-1_0.html#IDTokenValidation*

45 *http://openid.net/specs/openid-connect-basic-1_0.html#StandardClaims*

46 *http://openid.net/specs/openid-connect-registration-1_0.html*

experience is even more prominent than on the desktop. In the following chapter, we discuss current multifactor authentication systems and viable alternatives, such as biometrics, to identify users and grant authorization for certain actions or information.

CHAPTER 5

Alternate Methods of Identification

Tim Messerschmidt and Jonathan LeBlanc

Because of the heavy intersection between mobile devices, desktop clients, and a new breed of connected hardware out of the Internet of Things, the demand for a new class of authentication and authorization technology is on the rise. This chapter covers upcoming standards such as FIDO (*http://fidoalliance.org*) that enable covering multiple form factors and are able to scale beyond software-based authentication technology.

Device and Browser Fingerprinting

Next to regular authentication and authorization scenarios, device and browser fingerprinting allows for a more passive way to identify users across a big target group. Applications like Am I Unique? (*http://amiunique.org*) are broadly available and can leverage many factors in order to determine whether a user is unique.

When performing device and browser fingerprinting, the user is usually tested against some very general and broad factors—such as the device's platform, the current browser, or whether cookies are enabled on the device—and then against more granular and subtle determinants, like the device's resolution, time zone, the browser's enabled plug-ins, or user agent. When Flash is enabled, services like Am I Unique? or Panopticlick (*http://panopticlick.eff.org*) are even able to obtain a list of currently installed fonts.

Eight factors can be concatenated and lead to a browser's fingerprint (Table 5-1).

Table 5-1. Browser measurements to determine uniqueness

Variable	Obtained through
User Agent	HTTP
HTTP ACCEPT headers	HTTP
Cookies enabled	HTTP
Screen resolution	AJAX
Timezone	AJAX
Browser plugins	AJAX
System fonts	Flash or Java applets, collected through AJAX
Supercookie test	AJAX

Additional factors, such as the user's geolocation, can be obtained through HTML5 if the user agrees to share them or by analyzing the user's IP address (which does not require the user's consent).

Panopticlick released a paper on browser uniqueness that is a worthwhile read and a great source for further information on this subject.[1]

Two-Factor Authentication and n-Factor Authentication

Because of the known weaknesses and issues that come along with basic authentication through passwords, the demand for more secure login methods is high. Two-factor authentication (2FA) relies on the addition of another token, such as a one-time password, which is consumed after usage and therefore prevents common security exploits, such as replay attacks. This section explains the basic concepts of both two-factor authentication and the upcoming n-factor authentication technologies.

n-Factor Authentication

n-factor authentication, also known as *multifactor authentication* (MFA), is based on assuming that every individual should have three basic components:

- Something you know
- Something you have
- Something you are

---

[1] *http://panopticlick.eff.org/browser-uniqueness.pdf*

When examining these three requirements, you will quickly realize that they match concepts that we have discussed before. *Something you know* is the most basic component and can be assumed as granted: it can be as simple as a password or passphrase.

The second item on our list, *something you have*, aims at securing passwords or passphrases by adding another layer of protection. Popular examples are smart cards or RSA Tokens, which are used for RSA's SecurID network authentication technology. As of 2014 about 1.75 billion people worldwide have access to mobile phones—a small and affordable piece of technology that can easily act as an additional physical layer in authentication and authorization technology.[2] By being able to receive text messages and/or emails and allowing for the installation of authentication applications that generate one-time passwords, such as Google Authenticator (*http://github.com/google/google-authenticator*) and Authy (*http://www.authy.com*), people are able to secure existing logins.

Lastly, *something you are* focuses on the individual's identity and adds a handful of new challenges that we discuss in the following section. The basic assumption here is that the usage of something intrinsic, such as the individual's fingerprint, uniquely identifies the user among all users and therefore adds a third layer of security.

One-Time Passwords

One-time passwords, known as *OTPs*, have been positioned in the industry as a means to fight traditional password weaknesses and exploits. By being ever-changing and usable only once, they reduce an application's attack surface drastically.

Currently, there are three ways to generate one-time passwords. The first implementation, time-synchronization, generates short-lived tokens. Popular two-factor authentication applications, such as Authy or Google Authenticator, use this method to generate OTPs.

Both the second and third implementations are based on mathematical algorithms and generate long-lived tokens. One way to handle these OTPs is generating them based on the previous password, and therefore requiring them to be used in a predefined order. The other way to handle mathematically generated OTPs is generating them based on a random challenge.

When not being generated by a client-side application, OTPs can be delivered by either text messages or emails. The industry tends to favor text over email at the moment because it's broadly available; a phone number is rated to be unique across all users, and can be made accessible through text-to-speech and therefore also cover landline phones. A reason to use emails instead is the cost of sending a text message

---

2 *http://www.emarketer.com/Article/Smartphone-Users-Worldwide-Will-Total-175-Billion-2014/1010536*

and the inability to check whether the text message arrived at its destination. Another issue of text messages is the weak (A5/x) or nonexistent encryption standards that allow for man-in-the-middle attacks.[3]

On mobile devices, using emails to transport one-time passwords has one big advantage for the user experience: applications can automatically open and import the OTP, which heavily reduces friction and is being used by companies like Slack (Figure 5-1). The key to automating this process is registering a custom URL handler (via Android's application manifest[4] and utilizing URL Schemes on iOS[5]) that detects when URLs of a certain markup are handled.

Figure 5-1. Slack's mobile sign-in flow

---

3 http://www.cs.technion.ac.il/users/wwwb/cgi-bin/tr-get.cgi/2006/CS/CS-2006-07.pdf

4 http://stackoverflow.com/a/2448531/636579

5 http://code.tutsplus.com/tutorials/ios-sdk-working-with-url-schemes—mobile-6629

This sign-in flow results in an email similar to the one shown in Figure 5-2.

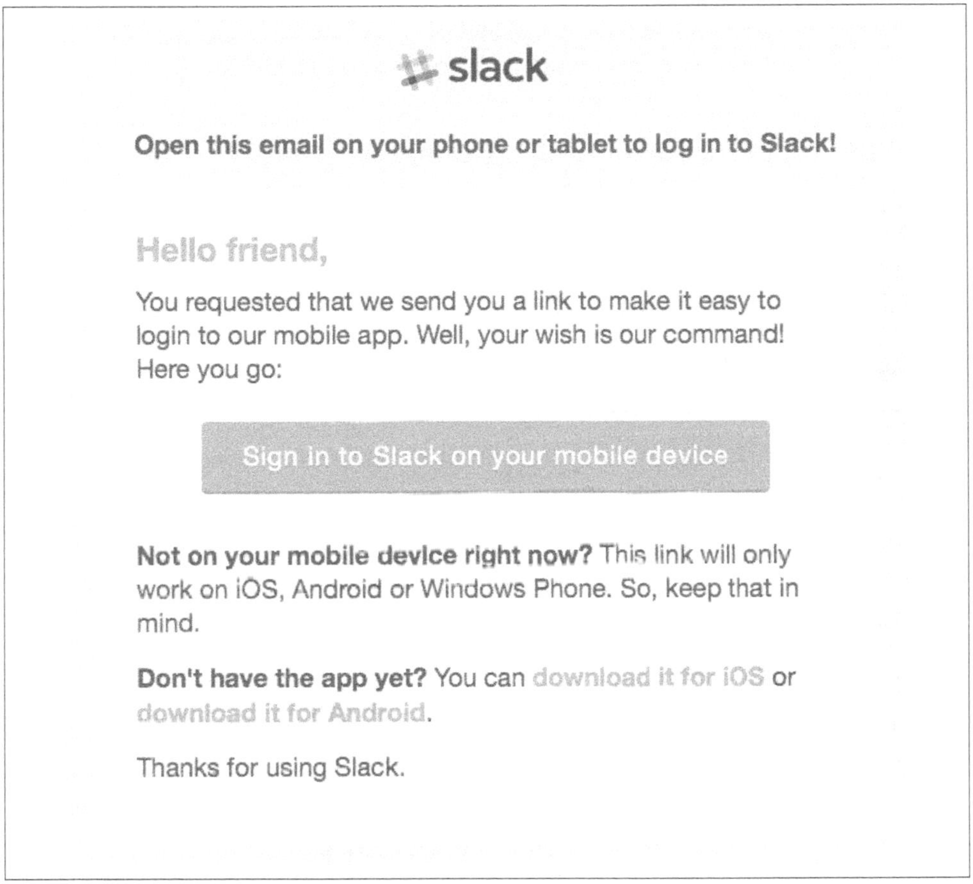

Figure 5-2. Slack's sign-in email for mobile devices

When analyzing the email's source code, you'll notice that a URL like the following is used: *https://slack.com/z-app-211=9624547-19991285158-c]1DJfjfFa?s=3Dslack.* Because Slack clearly owns the authority over slack.com (and no other applications *should* claim any URIs containing this domain), no custom scheme workaround like myapp://auth.com/ is needed. By clicking the "Sign in to Slack on your mobile device" button from within your mobile email client, you open the Slack application and will be signed in.

Since version 6.0 (Marshmallow), Android enables declaring website associations.[6] This mechanism helps to protect your native applications by preventing third-party applications from accessing information that is meant for internal consumption only.

Implementing Two-Factor Authentication with Authy

Now that you understand how OTPs work, let's see how to implement these within our own apps and websites. For this example, we're going to use a Twilio authentication service called Authy (*https://www.authy.com*). Authy will allow us to do things that we'll need for a 2FA system, such as the following:

- Register/delete 2FA user accounts on our service.
- Send SMS verification codes to those users.
- Verify the verification codes after users enter them on the website to verify themselves.

With that said, our first task is to set up an application with Authy and get a key that we will use to verify our application against the service. We can do that by following these steps:

1. Go to the Authy dashboard at *https://dashboard.authy.com/signin*.
2. Sign in or register a new account.
3. Click Access Authy Dashboard.
4. Click Enable Two-Factor Authentication, and select your preferred verification method, which is required to create a new application.
5. Click Create Your First App.
6. Enter an application name on the form that pops up; then click Create. Follow the rest of the instructions to create the application.

Once the application dashboard comes up, at the top of the page you will see an information section, which includes your hidden product and sandbox keys. We're going to be using our production key, so click the eye beside the hidden key to reveal it (Figure 5-3).

---

6 *http://developer.android.com/training/app-links/index.html#web-assoc*

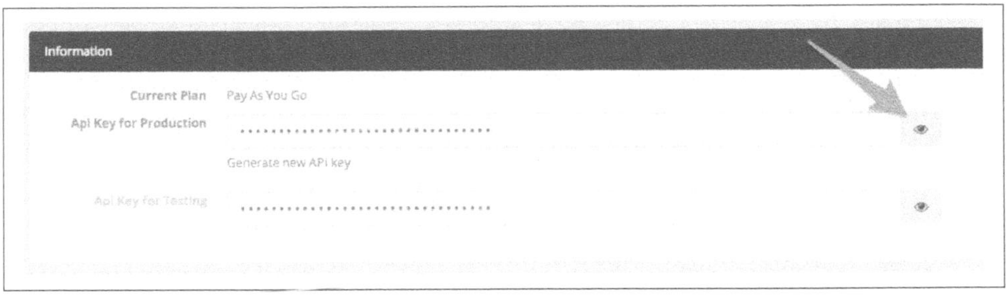

Figure 5-3. Authy key details

Take note of that key, because we'll be using it in our Authy 2FA example.

> The complete sample code for the following Authy example is available at *https://github.com/iddatasecuritybook/chapter5/tree/master/authy-2fa*.

With our key in hand, let's dive into a practical walk-through of how to implement 2FA using the service. First we need to install a few npm modules, specifically:

body-parser (https://www.npmjs.com/package/body-parser)
   For dealing with JSON/URL-encoded payloads post Express 4.0

authy (https://www.npmjs.com/package/authy)
   A helpful module for working with Authy functionality for users and tokens

We can pull down these packages via npm with the following terminal commands:

```
npm install body-parser --save
npm install authy --save
```

We can now create our *.js* file, and instantiate our packages and the body-parser functionality:

```
var express = require('express'),
    app = express(),
    bodyParser = require('body-parser'),
    authy = require('authy')('YOUR AUTHY PRODUCTION API KEY');

//to support JSON-encoded bodies
app.use(bodyParser.json());
//to support URL-encoded bodies
app.use(bodyParser.urlencoded({ extended: true }));
```

In the preceding code, we set up our express, body-parser, and authy variables. With the Authy instantiation, we pass in that Authy production key that we obtained when we created our application on the site. In the last two lines, we then set up body-parser to be able to handle JSON- and URL-encoded objects that we will need to parse from our requests later.

With Express, we can now set up a few routes in our application to handle POST requests to different endpoints for working with user setup and token verification. Let's start with defining a route to handle user registration:

 When should you register a new user with Authy?

The Authy registration for new users should be done when you have a new user creating an account with your site or service, during your regular registration process. As you are storing user information for your site, you will also store the user ID that Authy provides during registration.

```
//route: register a new user via provided email and phone number
app.post('/register', function(req, res){
    var email = req.body.email;
    var number = req.body.number;

    authy.register_user(email, number, function (err, response){
        //expected response:
        //{ message: 'User created successfully.',
        //   user: { id: 16782433 },
        //   success: true }
        res.send(response);
    });
});
```

The preceding route will allow any POST request sent to the /register endpoint of the application to be handled. The endpoint is expecting two pieces of data to be sent to it:

email
    The email of the user to be registered. This should match the email that was stored in your user records when you registered the individual.

number
    The phone number of the user to be used for the SMS 2FA process.

With that information obtained, we then make a request to authy.regis ter_user(…), passing in the email and number that we just pulled from the POST body. If all is successful, the return value (stored in response), should contain three pieces of data:

message
    The human-readable success message.

user

> The user ID of the newly registered user. This should be stored in your user database for sending the 2FA requests.

success

> A Boolean true/false indicating the success state.

Next on our list is to set up the ability to send SMS 2FA messages to a given user ID:

When should you send the SMS verification code?

SMS verification should be conducted during login. When a user enters her first set of credentials (typically username/password), you can then send the SMS message from Authy for a second level of authentication.

```
//route: send authy SMS message with verification code
app.post('/sms', function(req, res){
    var uid = req.body.uid;

    authy.request_sms(uid, function (err, response){
        //expected response:
        //{ success: true,
        //  message: 'SMS token was sent',
        //  cellphone: '+1-XX12362760' }
        res.send(response);
    });
});
```

This route will accept any POST request to the /sms endpoint, and will expect one piece of data to be POSTed:

uid

> The user ID that was obtained from registering the user with Authy, during the last step.

Once we pull out that value, we can then make a request to authy.request_sms(...), passing along that UID and a callback. This will attempt to send an SMS verification code to the phone number that is registered for that given user during the registration step. In the response object (on success), we are expecting a few parameters:

success

> A Boolean true/false indicating the success state

message

> The human-readable success message

```
cellphone
```
The cell phone number that the SMS was transmitted to

At this point, the user has obtained a verification code. She will enter the code on your site, and you will need to verify that it is correct:

How and when should you validate a verification code?

When users are sent the SMS verification code during the login step (for second factor verification), you should supply a method for them to enter the code that they see on their mobile device on your site.

```
//route: verify a provided verification token against a given user
app.post('/verify', function(req, res){
    var uid = req.body.uid;
    var token = req.body.token;

    authy.verify(uid, token, function (err, response){
        //expected response:
        //{ message: 'Token is valid.',
        //  token: 'is valid',
        //  success: 'true' }
        res.send(response);
    });
});
```

This route will handle the verification step. It will accept a POST request to the /verify endpoint, and will expect two pieces of data in the POST body:

```
uid
```
The user ID that Authy provided during the registration step

```
token
```
The verification token that the user was sent via SMS during the last step

Once we obtain that information, we can then call authy.verify(...), passing in the UID, token, and a callback function. If the verification step completes successfully, we can expect three pieces of data to come back from the response:

```
message
```
The human-readable success message

```
token
```
Verification of whether the token is valid

```
success
```
A Boolean true/false indicating the success state

Once we verify the token is legitimate, we can then allow the user to enter the site, and the 2FA process is now complete.

If a user deletes her account from our site we may need a last step. We want to ensure that we clean up all residual user information, including her Authy user registration data:

When should you delete users from Authy?

When users delete their account with your site or service, you should also clean up their information in Authy by deleting the registered account. The registration/deletion steps should be synced with your site/service registration and deletion steps.

```
//route: delete an existing user
app.post('/delete', function(req, res){
    var uid = req.body.uid;
    authy.delete_user(uid, function (err, response){
        //expected response:
        //{ message: 'User was added to remove.', success: true }
        res.send(response);
    });
});
```

This route will accept a POST request to the /delete endpoint, and expect one item in the POSTed data:

uid
   The user ID that Authy provided during the registration step

When obtained, we then make a call to authy.delete_user(…), passing along the user ID and a callback. If the deletion is successful, we should see the following parameters come back in the response:

message
   The human-readable success message

success
   A Boolean true/false indicating the success state

Once done, the user has been removed from the Authy registration system. In our app sample, the last thing we need to do is start the server:

```
app.listen(process.env.PORT || 3000);
```

This will listen on the expected port (such as if running via Heroku), or on port 3000 otherwise. Once the server is up and running (assuming on localhost port 3000 in this case), we can then run some tests by sending POST requests from the terminal to each of the endpoints we set up.

First we issue a request to register a new user:

```
curl -H "Content-Type: application/json" -X POST -d
'{"email":"jenny@email.com, "number":"18675309"}' http://localhost:3000/register
```

We send an HTTP POST request to the `register` endpoint, passing along an email and phone number in the POST body. The JSON response from that will give us the user ID for the newly registered person, which we will use for the next step.

The second step is to trigger the send of an SMS to the phone of that registered user:

```
curl -H "Content-Type: application/json" -X POST -d
'{"uid":"16572253"}' http://localhost:3000/sms
```

From the registration request, we obtained a user ID from Authy. We send that UID through to the SMS endpoint. The response should be a text message showing up on the registered phone number. The response from that will provide us with a verification code via SMS.

Next, we send the token we have in our SMS through for verification:

```
curl -H "Content-Type: application/json" -X POST -d
'{"uid":"16572253", "token":"0512278"}' http://localhost:3000/verify
```

We send the user ID and token via a POST body to the `/verify` endpoint, which should provide us with a message stating that the token is valid, if the request was successful.

The last step is to clean up the user records by deleting the user we just created:

```
curl -H "Content-Type: application/json" -X POST -d
'{"uid":"16572253"}' http://localhost:3000/delete
```

We send the user ID to the `/delete` endpoint, which, on success, will provide us with a success message response.

With all of that in place, we now have the structure to provide 2FA SMS token verification for our users.

Biometrics as Username Instead of Password

With the growing availability of fingerprint scanners on mobile devices, such as the iPhone device family and newer Android devices, more and more applications are trying to identify use cases that enhance the overall user experience. This surge in new technology has led to people wanting to use their fingerprint to replace password prompts on their phones.

From a logical standpoint, it might seem an easy choice to leverage biometrics to authorize access to applications, unlock a device's screen, and much more, but this creates new issues. Passwords are traditionally vulnerable, as we discussed in Chapters 1 and 2, and can be leaked or exposed to third parties. When using simple passwords, we can simply alter that password and exchange it for a new, more secure one. When using fingerprints, we run into a whole new dimension of issues: human beings have a maximum of ten fingers, and it is highly desirable that those fingerprints are not invalidated by being exposed to the public.

Using Fingerprints as a Security Mechanism

The German Chaos Computer Club managed to bypass the security mechanisms of Apple's TouchID in 2013. By replicating a fingerprint using a high-resolution photograph, the CCC managed to trick an iPhone 5s TouchID sensor into unlocking the phone. In the exploit's summary, the CCC highly recommends not using fingerprints to secure anything.[7]

Tim Bray, co-inventor of XML and contributor to the IETF's OAuth work, expressed his opinion about using fingerprint scanners and other biometric factors in a blog post[8] that led to an interesting discussion with John Gruber, inventor of the Markdown standard.[9] Gruber states that using a fingerprint is still better than using no security (like not locking your phone with a four-digit pin or a passphrase) or weak security.

Considering the discussion between Bray and Gruber and the fact that the CCC managed to exploit fingerprint scanners into unlocking, it might be wise to consider biometric factors less as a security mechanism and more as a mechanism to prove identity.

How to Rate Biometric Effectiveness

When handling biometric factors for authentication scenarios, the false-positive rate, also known as false-acceptance rate, of the used mechanism is critical. Google requires third-party manufacturers that want to implement fingerprint scanners for Android phones to use an implementation that leads to a false-positive rate of not higher than 0.002%.[10] False-rejection, another confounding factor, leads to user frustration and should be avoided—Google's guidelines define a maximum rate of 10% and a maximum latency between scan and action of 1 second. A third important criterion to secure fingerprint scanning is limiting the number of false attempts before

---

7 http://www.ccc.de/en/updates/2013/ccc-breaks-apple-touchid

8 https://www.tbray.org/ongoing/When/201x/2013/09/22/The-Fingerprint-Hack

9 https://twitter.com/gruber/status/381857717406560257

10 https://static.googleusercontent.com/media/source.android.com/en//compatibility/android-cdd.pdf

disabling fingerprint scanning; Apple allows for three false attempts on iOS devices before asking the user to unlock the phone differently, while Google defines a maximum of five tries before disabling fingerprint scanning for at least 30 seconds (per the manufacturer's guideline).

Face Recognition

Facial recognition aims at using either digital images or videos to identify people. This process extracts and processes a wide array of so-called landmarks and features in order to match profiles. Factors such as the relative position and size of those landmarks are normalized and compared using either geometric (comparing distinguishing features) or photometric (generating statistical values) approaches. Emerging three-dimensional recognition systems have proven to be less sensitive to changes in lighting and can help improve recognition by scanning different angles (often at the same time, by stacking multiple sensors on the same chip).

Various banks such as the national banks of Costa Rica and Ecuador have announced that they will use facial recognition technology on mobile devices to secure access to banking accounts.[11] Alipay, the Alibaba Group's online payment platform, announced in November 2015 it will roll out facial recognition to both iOS and Android devices.[12] Both examples demonstrate that the finance industry does not seem to be completely behind fingerprint technology and tries to evaluate other biometric factors on a broader scale.

Retina and Iris Scanning

In a similar fashion to face recognition, retina scans rely on identifying unique patterns. When observing a person's eye, blood vessels can be analyzed to identify users (Figure 5-4). Even identical twins do not share the same blood-vessel network and therefore cannot circumvent this security concept.[13]

While both retina and iris scanning use cameras to identify people, the key difference lies in the identification process itself. Whereas retina scans rely on light being absorbed by blood vessels in order to analyze a person's retina, iris scanning takes an image of an eye that is then analyzed to identify structure. These images can be captured from a distance of 3 to 10 inches and therefore are considered less intrusive than retina scans that require the the user's eye to be much closer to the scanning device. An

---

11 *http://www.biometricupdate.com/201601/facephi-facial-recognition-solution-to-authenticate-banco-nacional-of-costa-rica-clients*

12 *http://findbiometrics.com/alipay-facial-recognition-comes-to-ios-android-212227/*

13 *http://blog.m2sys.com/biometric-hardware/iris-recognition-vs-retina-scanning-what-are-the-differences/*

iris is supposed to have 266 unique spots that can be leveraged to determine uniqueness.[14]

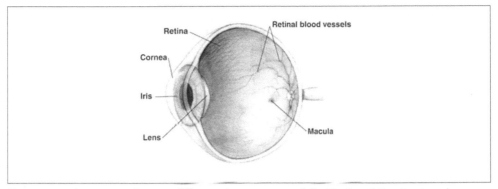

Figure 5-4. Anatomy of an eye (illustration courtesy of the National Eye Institute)

While a person's retina might change because of temporal or permanent effects (like diabetes or high blood pressure), the retina supposedly stays the same between the birth and death of a human being.[15]

Vein Recognition

While fingerprints remain usable as long as they can be duplicated or obtained in any other way, a person's veins are viable for authentication mechanisms only as long as blood flows through the body. Fujitsu has deployed palm vein recognition as a solution across ATMs in Japan that leverages biometric details to encrypt the dataset itself and therefore removes the need for encryption keys.[16]

Upcoming Standards

When analyzing the current authentication and authorization standards, it becomes quite apparent that the industry has not decided on a common standard. In this section, we present three currently viable contenders with very different focus and industry backing: The FIDO Alliance, Oz, and the Blockchain.

---

14 *http://www.globalsecurity.org/security/systems/biometrics-eye_scan.htm*

15 *http://blog.m2sys.com/biometric-hardware/iris-recognition-vs-retina-scanning-what-are-the-differences*

16 *http://www.biometricupdate.com/201510/fujitsu-laboratories-develops-method-to-convert-biometric-data-into-cryptographic-key*

FIDO Alliance

The *FIDO Alliance*, which stands for *Fast Identity Online*, is a new industry alliance between major contributors such as Google, BlackBerry, Microsoft, PayPal, and Lenovo. FIDO provides a scalable identity solution for multiple platforms and covers the three basic principles of authentication—*something you have, something you know, something you are*—by providing two scenarios: Universal Authentication Framework (UAF) and Universal 2nd Factor (U2F).

Both U2F and UAF are compatible with current federated identity services such as OpenID, SAML, and authorization protocols like OAuth.

UAF

UAF was designed with passwordless and mutlifactor authentication flows in mind. A trust relation is established by leveraging local mechanisms, such as using microphone input, entering a PIN, or fingerprint-scanning. The beauty of the protocol is that various factors can be combined; this kind of *security-layering* is a concept that is outlined in Chapter 6.

From a privacy perspective, the FIDO alliance dictates that only the minimal data needed should be collected, and used only for FIDO purposes. User verification is handled locally on the device and does not convey any biometric details to third parties (Figure 5-5).

Figure 5-5. FIDO UAF authentication

U2F

While UAF combines various factors to provide a secure and passwordless solution, U2F augments an existing authentication implementation by adding a second factor. The second factor simplifies password requirements to four-digit PIN codes and manifests in a device that presents the second factor via USB or NFC. This piece of hardware is usable across all implementing online services as long as the web browser supports the U2F protocol.

The devices are supposed to be designed with mainstream adoption in mind. This is why the design principles are minimal and allow for affordable hardware that can be distributed widely. From a security perspective, a secure key will be provided to manufacturers of secure elements and will change with every chipset batch.

U2F was designed with flexibility in mind: multiple people can share one device, and each person can use multiple devices to secure accounts across implementing sites (Figure 5-6).

Figure 5-6. FIDO U2F authentication

U2F utilizes a special registration and authentication message format to communicate with all supporting devices and browsers. Table 5-2 lists the requirements for the authentication message.

Table 5-2. Authentication message format

Parameter	Description
Control byte	0x07 to check if the key handle was created for the provided application parameter, 0x03 if a real signature and user presence is required
Challenge	SHA-256 hash of client data (stringified JSON)
Application	SHA-256 hash of the application identifier
Key handle length byte	Defines the length of the following key handle
Key handle	Provided by the relying party and obtained during registration

In case of a successful authentication, the response contains a parameter that provides information about the user presence, a counter that increments whenever a successful authentication operation was performed, and a signature consisting of the following:

- Application parameter (32 bytes)
- User presence byte (1 byte)
- Counter (4 bytes)
- Challenge parameter (32 bytes)

Oz

Eran Hammer, known for his contributions to both OAuth 1.0 and 2.0, published a web authorization framework called Oz (*http://github.com/hueniverse/oz*) in September 2015. This framework compiles industry best practices to provide not just a protocol but a concrete implementation that is opinionated about details such as client-side cryptography using HMAC.

This framework does not try to be a solution that covers all platforms and form factors, but rather a viable tool for JavaScript-based applications that aim to implement a secure solution for authorization.

Oz provides an OAuth 1.0-esque authorization flow and is based on two current solutions: Hawk (*https://github.com/hueniverse/hawk*), a client-server authorization protocol, and Iron (*https://github.com/hueniverse/iron*), a tool that allows encoding and verifying JavaScript objects. As opposed to OAuth, Oz tries not to handle user authentication; its sole purpose is handling application-to-server-authorization scenarios. From an architecture standpoint, Oz is similar to a slimmed-down implementation of OAuth 2 enriched with security best practices.

The Blockchain

Developed to verify Bitcoin transactions, the blockchain is slowly becoming a powerful tool beyond the scope of cryptocurrency and the payment landscape. The idea behind using the blockchain for identity scenarios is simple: a user can store proof of certain attributes—such as first and family name, address, or date of birth—and make the cryptographic hash of these attributes publicly available to anyone who is able to provide the user's public key. This allows individuals to verify information, while authenticity of these details can be ensured. The interesting twist in this concept is the ability to decide which pieces of information to share.

Let's use the example of a car accident. Somebody scratches our car and wants to provide important information such as insurance details, contact name, and phone number. We can only hope that the person gives us the correct details because we cannot verify anything until it is probably too late. Utilizing the blockchain, we could rely on exchanging cryptographic hashes and verify all information provided on the spot.

A company called ShoCard (*http://www.shocard.com*) tries to build upon this concept by providing a consumer-friendly mobile application. All information is stored in the public blockchain data layer (*http://www.shocard.com/what-is-a-blockchain*) and made accessible on demand.

Wrap Up

In this chapter, we explored upcoming standards and technologies that will provide simpler authentication flows and promise better security. In contrast, the following chapter provides an overview about currently available browser technology, Node modules, and integral server components that vastly enhance security and help us, the developers, build better applications.

CHAPTER 6

Hardening Web Applications

Tim Messerschmidt

We've spent some time in previous chapters discussing the relevance of OAuth 2.0 and OpenID Connect, and analyzed the relevance of identity and biometry plus the impact of multifactor authentication. This chapter covers security considerations for Node applications, especially focusing on Express.

In security, it is fantastic to provide a secure solution to identify users and authorize access to certain resources, but because of a multitude of attack vectors, it is simply not enough to rely on a simple protocol to secure applications. This is why we tend to go for layered security. Let's use a simple analogy: In medieval times, a castle was secured by a wooden gate, which was a good way to keep people out and defend property. When combined with stone walls, the gate got even better, because it took more time for even heavy machinery to breach the walls. If combined with a moat, the wall and gate became even more useful. If we take this analogy and apply it to today's standards, we want to make sure not only that our application is capable of identifying users, but also that we can withstand a DDoS attack, secure our sessions, and prepare for potential XSS and CSRF attacks.

Securing Sessions

Sessions have a simple reason to exist: they persist user logins across various routes within our application without the need to re-authenticate the user by prompting for usernames and passwords over and over again. Just like passwords, sessions have to meet certain requirements in order to meet security expectations: session IDs should be unique, nonguessable, and nonsequential. Just like passwords, sessions benefit from long session IDs that decrease attack vectors.

Types of Sessions

Before we dive into the details of sessions and securing sessions on top of the mechanisms that Express provides by default, it is sensible to explore the differences between cookies and sessions (Figure 6-1) and what makes them interesting.

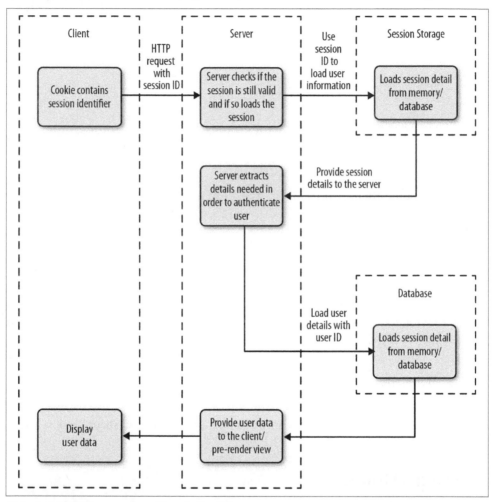

Figure 6-1. Session and cookie relationship

What's a cookie?

Cookies are used as client-side storage for information—they're mostly used in order to store certain user preferences, authentication details (such as the username and password), and session information. In fact, cookies can be seen as the client-side implementation of sessions and are usually combined with strong cryptographic mechanisms to provide safety, integrity, and authenticity of the data.

If you are looking for additional material on cookies, RFC 2965 "HTTP State Management Mechanisms" from 2000[1] states that cookies are not to be used for account information unless encryption is being used. Section 8 of the updated RFC 6265 from 2011[2] (this RFC supersedes RFC 2965) defines various considerations that must be taken into account to ensure security.

What's a session?

While cookies are used as a client-side mechanism, *sessions* are stored server side and serve as a way to persist user interaction with web applications. Session identifiers are used to handle a minimum of details on the client side but also expose the application to the possibility of session fixation attacks (as outlined in RFC 6265[3]).

How Express Handles Sessions

Since version 4 of Express, a lot of bundled middleware (for example, bodyParser, cookieParser, and session) has been moved into separate modules to allow for quicker updates and better maintainability. This section explores some of the functionality that the module express-session brings to the table in order to allow for secure handling of sessions.

When using the Express generator or looking at most tutorials, you will see a default initialization of the session middleware that looks something like this:

```
var session = require('express-session');

app.use(session({
  secret: 'mechagodzilla',
  resave: false,
  saveUninitialized: true,
  cookie: {
    secure: true
  }
}));
```

---

1 *http://tools.ietf.org/html/rfc2965*

2 *http://tools.ietf.org/html/rfc6265#section-8*

3 *http://tools.ietf.org/html/rfc6265#section-8.4*

Securing Passwords with SHA-2

SHA-256 is part of the family of SHA-2 (Secure Hash Algorithm) hash functions and produces digests (hash values) that are 256 bits by using 32-bit words. The SHA-2 finds usage in popular protocols such as SSL or PGP, but has recently received heavy criticism for being used as cryptographic tool in order to secure passwords. Please refer to Chapter 2 for additional information about SHA-2 and proper alternatives.

Let's look at the default options that are being passed to the middleware:

- `secret` is a required option and resembles the session secret that is utilized to sign the session ID cookie. The session module relies on the node module `cookie-signature`, which utilizes `crypto` (a popular module for cryptography) in order to sign the provided value with `SHA-256` as keyed-hash message authentication code, also known as HMAC. Finally, the signed value is hashed as `Base64` before being returned to Express.

- The next option, `resave`, determines whether sessions are saved in the session storage even when they did not get modified. This used to default to `true` but its use is no longer recommended. Instead, decide based on your session storage: if `req.session.touch()` is used, `resave` can be set to `false`; otherwise, `true` is the recommended value.[4]

- `saveUninitialized` is used to indicate whether a new (but unmodified) session should be saved. While `true` is the default value, it is recommend to set this value to `false` when being used to handle authentication.

- `cookie` allows for deeper configuration of your session ID cookie. `secure` is recommended to be set to `true` and ensures that secure cookies for HTTPS-enabled websites work. The session middleware does not rely on the `cookieParser` middleware anymore and can even cause issues when used in conjunction with it.

- `cookie.maxAge` is set to `null` by default and results in cookies being handled as browser-session cookies, which means that they are removed as soon as the browser window is closed.

---

4 *http://github.com/expressjs/session#resave*

Testing the session ID generation can be a difficult task when using the `secure` option for the cookie. The value `true` serves the cookie only via HTTPS. When testing on both HTTP and HTTPS connections, the value `auto` can be used, but please be aware that a cookie that is set via HTTPS is accessible only for HTTPS connections. Nonsecure cookies can be accessed using either HTTP or HTTPS.[5]

In our examples, we stick to `true` as the default value for our session cookie (this is the recommended setting).[6] When developing in a non-HTTPS-enabled environment, consider setting `secure` to `false`.

A prime feature of this middleware is the possibility of setting up your own function for generating session IDs. `genid` can be used with any function that creates and returns unique IDs. Currently, the default implementation uses `uid2`.

Using genid

While `uid2` seems to be a reasonable implementation for creating session IDs, `genid` provides a way to create harder-to-guess IDs, provide Access Tokens, or whichever other scenario you are looking for. Asynchronous functions are sadly not supported as of now but are a listed issue in the project's repository.[7]

Let's use `genid` to produce our own session IDs:

```
var session = require('express-session');
var uuid = require('node-uuid');

app.use(session({
  genid: function(req) {
    return uuid.v4()
  },
  secret: 'mechagodzilla',
  resave: false,
  saveUninitialized: false,
  cookie: {
    secure: true
  }
}));
```

In this example, we generate UUIDs with `node-uuid`. In the following section, we will have an in-depth look at applying this in practice.

---

5 *http://www.w3.org/Protocols/rfc2109/rfc2109*

6 *http://github.com/expressjs/session#cookie-options*

7 *http://github.com/expressjs/session/issues/107*

Best practices when dealing with sessions

Sessions are designed to have a finite lifespan and are supposed to expire by either being invalidated through the web application or simple cookie mechanics. Within our application, we can tie the generated session to a timespan and therefore easily validate whether the session should remain valid, is invalid, or should be invalidated. To minimize expensive database operations, it is reasonable to provide the session's creation date as an additional suffix in the session hash itself. This not only helps to reduce computing time, but also adds another factor to the generated hash and therefore acts as an additional security mechanism. A potential attacker deals not only with the session's ID, but also with a timestamp. To make session-guessing even harder, we can add additional factors into generating session hashes.

When using your own function to generate session IDs, you need to be aware that the session secret provided to Express is not being used (even though it is a required parameter). The module `cookie-signature` is easy to use and allows for the signing and unsigning of cookies:

```
var cookie = require('cookie-signature');

var value = 'test';
var secret = 'myamazingsecret';

var signedValue = cookie.sign(value, secret);
// signedValue is 'test.6L58yh6xptQIl6IyKA5GxGr63TRJwwxTNUYy6ui51Bk'

var unsignedValue = cookie.unsign(signedValue, secret);
// unsignedValue is 'test'
```

Let's apply these best practices to the session-generation function we've worked with before:

```
var session = require('express-session');
var uuid = require('node-uuid');

app.use(session({
  genid: function (req) {
    var timestamp = Date.now();
    var id = uuid.v4();
    var sessionId = id + '$' + timestamp;
    return sessionId;
  },
  secret: 'mechagodzilla',
  resave: false,
  saveUninitialized: false,
  cookie: {
    secure: true
  }
}));
```

In this example, the $ symbol is being used as a delimiter. By leveraging this syntax, we can easily identify the timestamp after we've retrieved the session's ID. Using this mechanism, we not only benefit from making session-guessing harder, but also have the power to check whether sessions are expired already by simply validating the timestamp:

```
var sessionParts = req.sessionID.split('$');
if (sessionParts.length === 2) {
  var timestamp = sessionParts[1];
  // Validate session
  ...
}
```

In this section, you've learned how the `express-session` module works, which methods and modules it uses, and how to build your own secure implementation of session ID generation in order to achieve security-layering and make session-guessing harder than before.

Handling XSS

Cross-site scripting is a popular attack that was briefly introduced in Chapter 4. XSS attacks are based on the fact that the browser trusts sites it visits, and therefore can be led toward executing malicious code. By injecting this code into other sites, it's distributed and either persisted or used for one-off attacks such as filling out forms within web applications.

The Three Types of XSS Attacks

When dealing with XSS prevention mechanisms, three attack methods become apparent:

- Persistent XSS
- Reflected XSS
- DOM-based XSS

Persistent XSS relies on malicious code being stored in a website's database. This results in the injected code being loaded over and over again and was a popular exploit in the early days of Internet forums.

Reflected XSS attacks originate from the original request and can be seen as one-time attacks that are returned in the server's response to the victim.

The last type, DOM-based XSS, is based on modifying client-side code and often attacks the URL's fragment identifier, which we know as the hash mark that normally serves for navigational purposes. Another example of DOM-based XSS is modifying entries in HTML5's LocalStorage; OWASP released a cheat sheet when dealing with HTML5 in order to assist with securing your application.[8]

Testing XSS Protection Mechanisms

In this section, we will explore how a basic reflected injection attack works and which mechanisms Node, HTTP, and the browsers put into place to prevent exploitation.

First we will generate a new project (using the Express generator) configured to be vulnerable. To get started, execute the following command in your terminal:

```
express xss
cd express
npm install .
```

This generates the initial setup for our application. After all modules are installed, we can start working on a basic user-registration feature—residing in *views/index.jade*—which accepts a first and last name and eventually displays these details on a simple profile page:

```
extends layout

block content
  h1 Registration
  form(method='POST', action='/register')
    fieldset
      legend Your details
      label(for='firstname') Firstname
      input(id='firstname', name='firstname', type='text')
      label(for='lastname') Lastname
      input(id='lastname', name='lastname', type='text')
      input(type='submit', value='Submit')
```

The form submits a POST request with the populated body to the route `/register`. In this step, we will add this new route declaration to our application (which you can find in *routes/index.js*):

```
router.post('/register', function(req, res) {
  var user = {
    firstname: req.body.firstname,
    lastname: req.body.lastname
  };

  res.render('profile', { user: user });
});
```

---

8 *http://www.owasp.org/index.php/HTML5_Security_Cheat_Sheet#Local_Storage*

For this example, we don't bother with storing user data and simply render another template, `profile`, with the POST request's details. The profile page is created by running the following command:

```
touch views/profile.jade
```

The following template displays the user's first name and last name by using Jade's buffered code mechanism:

```
extends layout

block content
  h1 Your Profile
  p= user.firstname
  p= user.lastname
```

Now that all the pieces are in place, we can run our first attempt at an XSS attack. Instead of submitting an innocent combination of first and last name, we want to abuse the last name in order to submit a script that loads another site:

```
<script>window.location="http://tme.coffee"</script>
```

Submitting the details populates the POST request's body like this:

```
{
  firstname: 'Tim',
  lastname: '<script>window.location="http://tme.coffee"</script>'
}
```

Now the basic assumption is that our profile page would simply render the information provided and therefore load the URL *http://tme.coffee* instead of displaying the last name.

Gladly, Jade escapes buffered code and therefore simply renders the output shown in Figure 6-2.

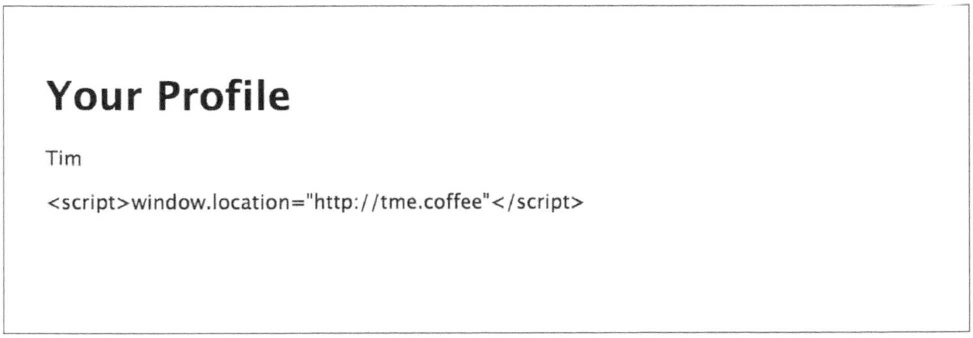

Your Profile

Tim

<script>window.location="http://tme.coffee"</script>

Figure 6-2. Escaped profile information

When inspecting the page's source, you will notice that the escaped profile page renders like this:

```
<body>
  <h1>Your Profile</h1>
  <p>Tim</p>
  <p>&lt;script&gt;window.location=
      &quot;http://tme.coffee&quot;&lt;/script&gt;</p>
</body>
```

For this upcoming step, let's be foolish and disable this automatic escaping-mechanism. We can do this by changing the template:

```
extends layout

block content
  h1 Your Profile
  p= user.firstname
  p!= user.lastname
```

Instead of displaying buffered code with =, we use the functionality to render unbuffered code, != (which is definitely not safe for input) and resubmit our form.

This is where things get interesting, as differences in browsers become quite apparent. Chrome (tested with Version 48.0.2564.48 beta) doesn't render the last name field and prints the following statement in the JavaScript console:

> The XSS Auditor refused to execute a script in *http://localhost: 3000/register* because its source code was found within the request. The auditor was enabled as the server sent neither an *X-XSS-Protection* nor *Content-Security-Policy* header.

Doing the same experiment with Mozilla's Firefox V42 results in the script tag executing—the browser loads up the page *http://tme.coffee*.

XSS Auditor is a feature that was initially introduced with WebKit and made its way into the Chromium Project's WebKit fork Blink. That implies that a wide array of browsers such as Chrome, Opera, and Safari come with this built-in mechanism against reflected XSS attacks. Microsoft's Internet Explorer supports XSS Auditor functionality with version 8 and above.

Circumventing XSS Auditor

XSS Auditor should not be seen as a sole defense mechanism against XSS attacks. It is rather an additional client-side tool to decrease the risk implied by vulnerable software. By blacklisting certain payloads and query parameters, injection points are supposed to be detected and execution on the browser DOM is prevented by transforming the response into a nonexecutable state.

Let's have a look at the script tag detection mechanism in WebKit's *XSSAuditor.cpp:*[9]

```
static bool startsOpeningScriptTagAt(const String& string, size_t start)
{
    return start + 6 < string.length() && string[start] == '<'
        && WTF::toASCIILowerUnchecked(string[start + 1]) == 's'
        && WTF::toASCIILowerUnchecked(string[start + 2]) == 'c'
        && WTF::toASCIILowerUnchecked(string[start + 3]) == 'r'
        && WTF::toASCIILowerUnchecked(string[start + 4]) == 'i'
        && WTF::toASCIILowerUnchecked(string[start + 5]) == 'p'
        && WTF::toASCIILowerUnchecked(string[start + 6]) == 't';
}
```

Based on this detection mechanism, potential threads can be detected and examined more deeply.

The Auditor relies on the following HTTP header to be set: X-XSS-Protection. We can inspect our request's header to understand how Express, Node, and Chrome handle this situation:

```
Accept:text/html,application/xhtml+xml,application/xml;q=0.9,image/webp,*/*;q=0.8
Accept-Encoding:gzip, deflate
Accept-Language:en-US,en;q=0.8,de;q=0.6
Cache-Control:max-age=0
Connection:keep-alive
Content-Length:73
Content-Type:application/x-www-form-urlencoded
Host:localhost:3000
If-None-Match:W/"be-JIAfZIOVAe1p85FawKqWIg"
Origin:http://localhost:3000
Referer:http://localhost:3000/
Upgrade-Insecure-Requests:1
User-Agent:Mozilla/5.0 (Macintosh; Intel Mac OS X 10_10_5) ...
```

The sample application does not provide the X-XSS-Protection itself; WebKit sets this option by default, and it needs to be explicitly disabled by setting the header manually:

```
router.post('/register', function(req, res) {
  var user = {
    firstname: req.body.firstname,
    lastname: req.body.lastname
  };

  res.set('X-XSS-Protection','0');
  res.render('profile', { user: user });
});
```

---

9 *https://github.com/WebKit/webkit/blob/fa65954cef5bc7a64f34e38d08f21833cad81506/Source/WebCore/html/parser/XSSAuditor.cpp#L102*

The header options value 0 disables this mechanism, 1 enables it, and 1;mode=block results in rendering a blank page. Obviously, it is always desirable to set the value to either 1 or 1;mode=block. Be aware that while other web frameworks—such as Sinatra for Ruby (*http://www.sinatrarb.com*)—provide the X-XSS-Protection header as default, Express relies on external modules such as Helmet (*http://www.npmjs.com/package/helmet*).

> Setting the X-XSS-Protection header causes vulnerabilities on old versions of Internet Explorer.[10] It is recommended to set the header to 0 accordingly. Helmet handles this exception automatically.[11]

Security consultant Egor Homakov wrote an interesting post about the mechanism of XSS Auditor.[12]

Conclusion

Through a combination of sensible browser defaults like the X-XSS-Protection header and the features of modern templating engines like escaping input, a solid base-layer security is being provided. Previously, we've explored security-layering, and it definitely makes sense to hold on to this behavior when dealing with reflected XSS. As developers, we should use both client-side and server-side features that help escaping and sanitizing input in order to prevent exploitation of our application.

More information on XSS attacks and tools that help with reducing attack vectors can be found on *http://excess-xss.com*.

CSRF Attacks

Nearly as popular as XSS, cross-site request forgery is used to leverage the browser's trust in a user to execute requests on the user's behalf. This can cause sites to execute requests that seemingly come from a valid authorized user and pose a huge threat. In fact, CSRF ranks as the eighth-biggest harm in OWASP's top 10 list of current security threats,[13] down from the fifth place in 2010.[14] While the threat might be decreasing in commonness, a place within the top 10 of ongoing vulnerabilities still justifies

---

10 *http://hackademix.net/2009/11/21/ies-xss-filter-creates-xss-vulnerabilities*

11 *http://github.com/helmetjs/helmet#xss-filter-xssfilter*

12 *http://homakov.blogspot.de/2013/02/hacking-with-xss-auditor.html*

13 *http://www.owasp.org/index.php/Category:OWASP_Top_Ten_Project#tab=OWASP_Top_10_for_2013*

14 *http://www.owasp.org/index.php/Category:OWASP_Top_Ten_Project#tab=OWASP_Top_10_for_2010*

discussing the issue itself and the prevention mechanisms that help Node.js developers to deploy secure applications.

Handling CSRF with csurf

Express offers an optional middleware called csurf (*http://github.com/expressjs/csurf*) that can be installed via npm. The module provides a unique token that needs to be rendered in forms and will be validated after form submission—a mechanism that's similar to what we have done with providing the state parameter when requesting the Authorization Code in the previous example:

```
var csurf = require('csurf');

var csrfMiddleware = csurf({
  cookie: true
});

app.get('/form', csrfMiddleware, function(req, res) {
  res.render('form', { csrfToken: req.csrfToken() });
});
```

In this example, we create a new middleware based on csurf that stores cookies instead of req.session to store the CSRF token secret. This middleware is mounted for the route /form and provides the generated token as an option to the form template:

```
extends layout

block content
  h1 CSRF protection using csurf
  form(action="/login" method="POST")
    input(type="text", name="username=", value="Username")
    input(type="password", name="password", value="Password")
    input(type="hidden", name="_csrf", value="#{csrfToken}")
    button(type="submit") Submit
```

By rendering the CSRF token as a hidden part of a hypothetical login form, we provide a way to send the token back to the server. This allows us to validate the authenticity of our request in the /login route:

```
app.post('/login', csrfMiddleware, function(req, res) {
  // This request is unique and can be handled accordingly
});
```

Some of the functionality in csurf relies on using a session middleware (like cookie-parser or express-session) before using the middleware itself. This is just a matter of handling the initialization process of your application's middleware accordingly.

Protecting our application against CSRF attacks with popular modules such as `csurf` is incredibly easy and leaves little excuse for not doing so. By simply using a middleware and handling the provided token, a whole level of threat can be managed.

Valuable Resources for Node

In this section, we briefly introduce a handful of Node modules that help you with improving your application's security.

Lusca

Back in 2012, PayPal started adopting Node to power its application stack. Part of this process was the development of krakenjs (*http://krakenjs.com*), an extension of Express. Part of the kraken suite is a module called Lusca, which focuses heavily on improving security by setting sensible defaults and providing protection mechanisms against prominent vulnerabilities.

Lusca can be used as application-level middleware by adding it to your application's initialization process:[15]

```
var express = require('express'),
    app = express(),
    session = require('express-session'),
    lusca = require('lusca');

//this or other session management will be required
app.use(session({
    secret: 'abc',
    resave: true,
    saveUninitialized: true
}));

app.use(lusca({
    csrf: true,
    csp: { /* ... */},
    xframe: 'SAMEORIGIN',
    p3p: 'ABCDEF',
    hsts: {maxAge: 31536000, includeSubDomains: true, preload: true},
    xssProtection: true
}));
```

Please note that not only common threats such as XSS and CSRF are covered. Lusca also features HTTP Strict Transport Security (HSTS), Content Security Policy (CSP) options, and support for the `X-Frame-Options` response header.

---

15 Sample taken from the project's documentation, *https://github.com/krakenjs/lusca#usage*

Helmet

Helmet (*http://github.com/helmetjs/helmet*) is a collection of 10 security middlewares that operate similarly to how PayPal's Lusca functions. You can either use a default initialization with `app.use(helmet())` and cover 6 out of 10 middlewares or use the submodules individually.[16]

Currently, Helmet comes with the following modules:

- `contentSecurityPolicy`, which contains CSP settings
- `dnsPrefetchControl`, which controls browser DNS prefetching. Currently beta and soon part of the default middleware.
- `frameguard`, for prevention of clickjacking
- `hidePoweredBy`, which controls the `X-Powered-By` header
- `hpkp`, HTTP Public Key Pinning
- `hsts`, HTTP Strict Transport Policy
- `ieNoOpen`, X-Download-Options (IE8 and newer)
- `noCache`, which enables or disables client-side caching
- `noSniff`, which prevents MIME-type sniffing
- `xssFilter`, the `X-XSS-Protection` header

We definitely recommend reading Helmet's documentation. The contributors took the time to provide detailed explanations of attack types and how they can be mitigated.[17]

Node Security Project

The last valuable resource that is worth mentioning is the Node Security Project. Subscribing to its Node Security Newsletter is definitely worthwhile and trying out nsp. nsp allows for auditing your Node application's *package.json* and *npm-shrinkwrap.json* files for known vulnerabilities.

Install nsp by running the following command:

```
npm install -g nsp
```

---

16 As documented in the project's repository, *http://github.com/helmetjs/helmet#how-it-works*

17 *http://github.com/helmetjs/helmet#usage-guide*

Then navigate to your project and run nsp like so:

```
cd testapp
nsp check
```

Potential output looks similar to Figure 6-3.

```
+  testapp  nsp check
(+) 2 vulnerabilities found
+------------+------------------------------------------------------------------+
|            | Regular Expression Denial of Service                             |
+------------+------------------------------------------------------------------+
| Name       | uglify-js                                                        |
+------------+------------------------------------------------------------------+
| Installed  | 2.2.5                                                             |
+------------+------------------------------------------------------------------+
| Vulnerable | <2.6.0                                                            |
+------------+------------------------------------------------------------------+
| Patched    | >=2.6.0                                                           |
+------------+------------------------------------------------------------------+
| Path       | testapp@0.0.0 > jade@1.11.0 > transformers@2.1.0 > uglify-js@2.2.5|
+------------+------------------------------------------------------------------+
| More Info  | https://nodesecurity.io/advisories/48                            |
+------------+------------------------------------------------------------------+

+------------+------------------------------------------------------------------+
|            | Incorrect Handling of Non-Boolean Comparisons During Minification|
+------------+------------------------------------------------------------------+
| Name       | uglify-js                                                        |
+------------+------------------------------------------------------------------+
| Installed  | 2.2.5                                                             |
+------------+------------------------------------------------------------------+
| Vulnerable | <= 2.4.23                                                         |
+------------+------------------------------------------------------------------+
| Patched    | >= 2.4.24                                                         |
+------------+------------------------------------------------------------------+
| Path       | testapp@0.0.0 > jade@1.11.0 > transformers@2.1.0 > uglify-js@2.2.5|
+------------+------------------------------------------------------------------+
| More Info  | https://nodesecurity.io/advisories/39                            |
+------------+------------------------------------------------------------------+
```

Figure 6-3. nsp security audit

The Node Security Project also curates a list of valuable resources (such as talks, papers, blog posts, and more).[18] This collection serves as a great overview of current security best practices for Node.

Other Mitigation Techniques

A lot of mitigation techniques—such as HSTS and CSP—have been mentioned in the preceding sections. Before moving on to the next chapter, Table 6-1 briefly summarizes their core functionality.

The X-Powered-By header does not necessarily open up a vulnerability but tells potential attackers about our application stack. By default, Express sets the header to X-Powered-By: Express and therefore exposes which framework was used to build the application. We recommend unsetting the header either by using the options provided by Helmet and Lusca, or manually as shown here:

---

18 *http://nodesecurity.io/resources*

```
router.get('/myroute', function(req, res) {
  res.set('X-Powered-By', '');
});
```

We highly recommend that you do some further research on these mitigtation techniques in order to understand how to implement them most effectively.

Table 6-1. Mitigation techniques

Mechanism	Description
Content Security Policy[a]	Prevents execution of malicious content in trusted sites (reduces risk of XSS).
HTTP Strict Transport Security[b]	A mechanism that allows applications to be accessed only via secure connections.
HTTP Public Key Pinning[c]	Ensures the authenticity of a server's public key.
Frameguard[d]	Allows you to define if an application can be framed (in a <frame> or <iframe> tag).
Platform for Privacy Preferences[e]	P3P defines which information a website collects about users.

[a] *http://content-security-policy.com*

[b] *http://tools.ietf.org/html/rfc6797*

[c] *https://developer.mozilla.org/en/docs/Web/Security/Public_Key_Pinning*

[d] *https://en.wikipedia.org/wiki/Clickjacking*

[e] *http://www.w3.org/P3P*

Our Findings

In this chapter, we have discussed and dissected session mechanisms, the potential threat behind cross-site scripting, and the severe impact of cross-site request forgery. So far you have learned about the following:

- Express security features (such as `express-session`)
- Client-side XSS prevention (XSS Auditor and the `X-XSS-Protection` header)
- Server-side XSS prevention (escaping and buffering parameters using templating engines)
- Securing requests against CSRF (providing unique tokens with `csurf`)
- Using security modules (`helmet` and `lusca`)
- Mitigation techniques (CSP, HSTS, HPKP, and more)

In the following chapter, we will look at efficient and secure data transmission using techniques such as SSL, asymmetric and symmetric encryption, and the implications of cryptography itself.

CHAPTER 7

Data Transmission Security

Jonathan LeBlanc

In Chapter 2, we discussed at length the protection of identification and account security through the use of proper hashing and salting techniques. Even though account security is vitally important to any system, what about security for any data that is being transmitted from one party to another, as that data might be sensitive in nature or contain privileged user information?

In this chapter, we explore numerous data-security techniques that are designed to protect data in motion, or better said, data that is moving between parties. We'll look at a few of these techniques in depth:

- SSL secure data transmission
- Asymmetric key cryptography, better known as public/private key encryption
- Symmetric key encryption, better known as shared secret encryption

Let's start out by exploring our ideal secure scenario.

SSL/TLS

In an ideal scenario, when working with data security as web developers, Secure Sockets Layer (SSL) is the mechanism that you should be targeting as your data security standard for a user. If you're not familiar with how it works, you'll be familiar with seeing the effect of an SSL certificate being used on websites that you visit, Figure 7-1, for example shows the expanded certificate information for *https:// www.google.com*.

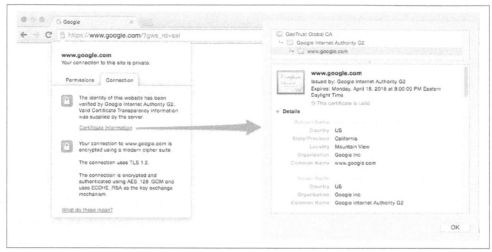

Figure 7-1. SSL certificate on Google

SSL, and its successor, Transport Layer Security (TLS), are cryptographic protocols that are typically bundled together. When creating a secure SSL connection on your website, you will be required to set up an SSL certificate provided by an SSL certificate authority (CA), which is a company that can issue these digital certificates. When doing so, you verify identification information about your site to the certificate authority, and then your web server generates two cryptographic keys: a public and a private key. This process uses the symmetric key cryptography approach to data security and data privacy, which we'll explore in more detail later in this chapter.

These certificates usually contain some basic information about you and your website:

- Domain name
- Company name
- Address
- City
- State/province
- Country

Certificate Validation Types and Authorities

You can obtain various SSL certificate types when working through a certificate authority, depending on your needs.

Domain Validation (DV)

The CA validates that the applicant has the right to use the specific domain name, meaning that someone with admin rights to the domain is aware of the application. Rights are typically proven by either receiving and confirming an email that is sent to the admin email for the domain, or by configuring specific DNS records for the domain. No company information is vetted or displayed to customers visiting the website who view the certificate details.

With domain validation, you will see the green lock in the URL bar, as shown in Figure 7-2, but will not see company-specific details when the certificate is loaded.

Figure 7-2. Domain validation certificate example

Organization Validation (OV)

The domain verification in the DV step is conducted, but in addition, the company/organization information goes through some vetting, such as name, city, state, and country. This basic information will also be displayed to customers visiting the website who view the certificate details.

With sites that have this type of validation, you will be able to see company information when the certificate is loaded, as shown in Figure 7-3.

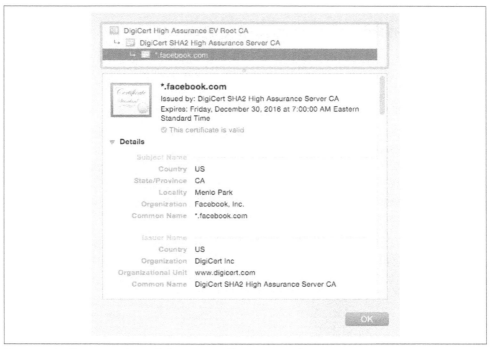

Figure 7-3. Organization validation certificate example

Extended Validation (EV)

The CA validates domain ownership (DA), organization information (OV), as well as checks the legal existence of the organization. This is the lengthiest process of the three, and also validates that the organization is aware of the SSL certificate request and approves it. The validation step requires specific documentation that certifies the identity of the company, as well as an additional set of steps and checks.

Typically, you will see an example of this type of validation in sites that have a green address bar with the lock and company name, as displayed in Figure 7-4.

Figure 7-4. Extended validation certificate example

When working with a CA, such as DigiCert, GoDaddy, Verisign, or Comodo you will typically be brought through a few steps to do the following:

- Create a certificate signing request (CSR)
- Purchase the certificate

Once the certificate is purchased, the CA will validate and process the CSR, and then issue you the certificate for installation (typically through email). Many CAs offer support for Wilcard certificates, which allow you to also secure all subdomains under a root domain.

Creating Your Own Self-Signed Certificate for Testing

Using in Production Will Produce an Error

Working with self-signed certificates, as you will see in this section, should never be done in a production environment where you are expecting actual traffic. The entire purpose of working with self-signed certificates is for testing only. Using them will produce a nasty browser warning explaining to all your visitors that your certificate is not trusted. You have been warned. The message looks like Figure 7-5, which will take over the entire browser window before going on to your site content.

Figure 7-5. Untrusted certificate warning

Now that you have been thoroughly warned about using the following section for testing only, let's proceed to create and sign our own certificates for testing purposes. This will allow us to build our infrastructure in a separate environment before moving to a proper production environment with a trusted certificate authority.

In the previous sections, you learned about the fundamentals of setting up a production-level certificate. Now let's go through the steps needed for setting up our own certificate.

Certificate setup

The first step is to create our private key and the self-signed certificate that we will be using when we spin up a Node server instance.

For the sake of the example, we're going to store our keys in the same folder as the program that we will be running. With that said, load up a terminal window and go to the folder you are using for this program.

Let's start with the private key setup. Type in the following command:

```
openssl genrsa -des3 -out server.key 2048
```

You will be asked to enter and verify a password for the file. What you are essentially doing is creating a new 2048-bit, triple-DES-encrypted RSA key; encrypting it with a password; and then storing it to a file, *server.enc.key*.

The process looks like Figure 7-6.

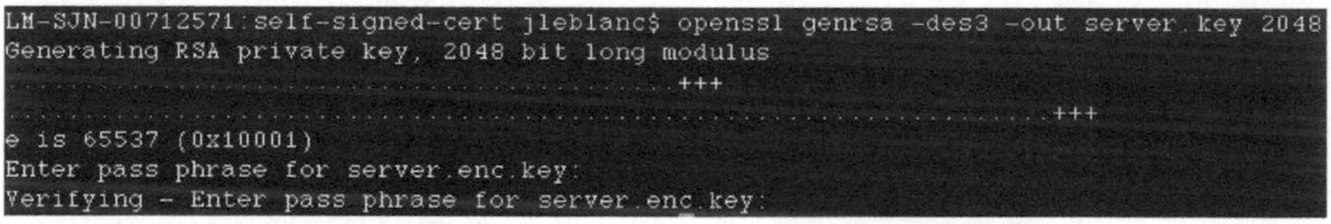

Figure 7-6. Generating a 2048-bit RSA key

Next up, we need to create a certificate signing request (CSR). Using our previously generated key, we issue the following command:

```
openssl req -new -key server.key -out server.csr
```

This will create our certificate signing request, with the intent of outputting the CSR to *server.csr*. After issuing the command, you will be required to input more detailed information about yourself and your company.

- The passphrase used for the private key (the same one used for the last command)
- Your two digit country code
- Your state or province
- Your city or locality name
- Your company or organization name
- The group or unit that this belongs to in the company

- Any common name to be used for the certificate request, or your name
- An appropriate email address to contact

You will also be asked to add a few extra attributes, including these:

- A challenge password
- A company name (optional)

The entire process, end-to-end, looks like Figure 7-7.

```
LM-SJN-00712571:self-signed-cert jleblanc$ openssl req -new -key server.key -out server.csr
Enter pass phrase for server.enc.key:
You are about to be asked to enter information that will be incorporated
into your certificate request.
What you are about to enter is what is called a Distinguished Name or a DN.
There are quite a few fields but you can leave some blank
For some fields there will be a default value,
If you enter '.', the field will be left blank.
-----
Country Name (2 letter code) [AU]:US
State or Province Name (full name) [Some-State]:Arizona
Locality Name (eg, city) []:Lake Havasu City
Organization Name (eg, company) [Internet Widgits Pty Ltd]:Acme Corporation
Organizational Unit Name (eg, section) []:Mail-Order Merchandise
Common Name (e.g. server FQDN or YOUR name) []:ACME
Email Address []:wileecoyote@acme.com

Please enter the following 'extra' attributes
to be sent with your certificate request
A challenge password []:greattunnelpainter
An optional company name []:Coyote Inc
```

Figure 7-7. Creating a certificate signing request

Removing Key Encryption

If you are using the self-signed certificate for testing and wish to remove the password and encryption from your private key (not recommended for anything but single-user, local testing), then at this point you could use your previously generated encrypted private key (say that's server.enc.key), and generate the new unencrypted private key (server.key) with the following command:

```
openssl rsa -in server.enc.key -out server.key
```

The list of commands to issue to get to the same point as we were in this section, using this method, are shown here:

```
openssl genrsa -des3 -out server.enc.key 2048
openssl req -new -key server.enc.key -out server.csr
openssl rsa -in server.enc.key -out server.key
```

Now that we have our CSR in place, we can self-sign the certificate to create our needed certificate file (CRT), using the following command:

```
openssl x509 -req -days 365 -in server.csr -signkey server.key -out server.crt
```

This command creates a temporary certificate for one year (specified by the -days option). If you did not remove the encryption from the original key file, then you will be required to enter the key passphrase for this step, as shown in Figure 7-8.

```
LM-SJN-00712571:self-signed-cert jleblanc$ openssl x509 -req -days 365 -in server.csr -signkey server.key -out server.crt
Signature ok
subject=/C=US/ST=Arizona/L=Lake Havasu City/O=Acme Corporation/OU=Mail-Order Merchandise/CN=ACME/emailAddress=wileecoyote@acme
.com
Getting Private key
Enter pass phrase for server.enc.key:
```

Figure 7-8. Creating the self-signed certificate

Our self-signed certificate is now ready for us to use in our server setup, to start creating secure HTTPS connections between the server and browser.

Server setup

 The server code for the following example is available in its entirety at *https://github.com/iddatasecuritybook/chapter7/blob/master/self-signed-cert/server.js*.

For the sake of our example server, we're going to assume that you chose not to remove the encryption from your private key in the last section, but we'll still go through how to adjust the code in case you no longer need the passphrase. We're also assuming that you have Express set up as we go through the code sample.

We're going to look at an Express server setup that will use our private key and self-signed certificate from the previous step to accept secure (HTTPS) connections from an alternate source, such as the browser or another program that we're running locally. In this case, we will be working with JSON strings that will be sent from another program to our server, through a secure communication channel thanks to our certificate and key.

We will be working with a few modules for our server, the filesystem (fs), https, and querystring, which are all standard modules and don't require pulling anything from npm, as well as body-parser, which will allow us to support JSON/URL-encoded bodies in Express 4.0 or beyond. We install body-parser from npm with the following command:

```
npm install body-parser --save
```

Let's look at the server code in its entirety, and then describe what's going on in each step:

```
var fs = require('fs'),
    https = require('https'),
    querystring = require('querystring'),
```

```
    bodyParser = require('body-parser')
    app = require('express')();

//support JSON & URL encoded bodies
app.use(bodyParser.json());
app.use(bodyParser.urlencoded({
    extended: true
}));

//handle all POST requests
app.post('/', function (req, res){
    var message = req.body;
    res.send('Message received:' + querystring.stringify(message));
});

//set certificate options
var options = {
    key: fs.readFileSync('server.key'),
    cert: fs.readFileSync('server.crt'),
    passphrase: 'YOUR KEY PASSWORD'
};

//create server with certificate options
https.createServer(options, app).listen(3000, function () {
    console.log('Server started: Listening on port 3000');
});
```

 In the code example, you can see that we refer to a passphrase and your key password as the input. These values should never be hard-coded in your code. Instead, you should use environment variables, files with restricted read permissions, or the like. The Node module dotenv is a great way to handle these environment variables. A complete run through of its use is available in "Application Configuration" on page 177.

We start off by including all of our required modules, then adding in our body-parser options to Express for supporting JSON- and URL-encoded strings. Those sections comprise our first two blocks of code.

Next we need to handle all incoming POST requests that will be coming to the server. We do that by setting app.post(/, …). In the return function, we first start by extracting req.body, which will be the POST object that the browser or other program sent over. In this example, we then simply send back an acknowledgment that the message was received.

In the next block, we set up our certificate options to create that secure connection. Within the `options` variable, we add three pieces of data:

key
> Our private key, read in from our local *server.key* file.

cert
> Our self-signed certificate, read in from our local *server.crt* file.

passphrase
> The passphrase for our private key file. If you removed the encryption from this key file in the previous section, you can omit this line.

Lastly, we create our server instance, with those options, and listen on port 3000. When you're ready to test this out, you can issue the following command on your terminal, assuming the file is saved as *server.js*:

```
node server.js
```

The server will spin up on port 3000 and will start listening for incoming traffic. Our next step is to set up another script to act as our client, and send it over an appropriate JSON object over our new HTTPS connection.

Making secure requests to the server

The client code for the following example is available in its entirety at *https://github.com/iddatasecuritybook/chapter7/blob/master/self-signed-cert/client.js*.

Our client script, *client.js*, is a fairly standard POST request, with a few differences. We'll look at the full code next, then describe each of the sections (and any caveats):

```
var querystring = require('querystring'),
    https = require('https');

//POST data to be sent to server
var postData = querystring.stringify({
    'message' : 'My secure JSON string'
});

//POST options
var postOptions = {
    hostname: 'localhost',
    port: 3000,
    path: '/',
    rejectUnauthorized: false,
    method: 'POST',
    headers: {
```

```
            'Content-Type': 'application/x-www-form-urlencoded',
            'Content-Length': postData.length
        }
    };

    //set up HTTPS POST request to server
    var postReq = https.request(postOptions, function(res){
        res.setEncoding('utf8');
        res.on('data', function (data){
            console.log(data);
        });
    });

    //POST data to server
    postReq.write(postData);
    postReq.end();
```

We start things off by including the `querystring` and `https` standard Node modules.

We then create the JSON object that we will be sending through the HTTPS POST request, `post_data`. We add just a simple string for our needs, then stringify the entire object for POSTing.

Under the POST options, this is where we need to pay attention to slight differences from a standard POST request with a non-self-signed certificate. Within the POST options, we specify a few options:

hostname
> The host to send the request to. Because we're running the server locally, this is localhost.

port
> The port to make the request to. The server is on port 3000, so that's what we specify here.

path
> The path to make the request to. The server is accepting all POST traffic to the same handle, so this can be anything.

rejectUnauthorized
> This is the one to take note of. Specifying this as `false` will allow you to make POST requests with a self-signed certificate without being blocked by a certificate error.

method
> The HTTPS request method, in this case POST.

headers
> Our content headers, specifying content type and length.

Adding `rejectUnauthorized: false` to your POST options will allow you to work with a self-signed certificate without receiving error messages about the certificate not being trusted. The error produced, when not properly handled, will throw an error much like Figure 7-9.

```
LM-SJN-00712571:self-signed-cert jleblanc$ node client.js
events.js:141
      throw er; // Unhandled 'error' event
      ^

Error: self signed certificate
    at Error (native)
    at TLSSocket.<anonymous> (_tls_wrap.js:1000:38)
    at emitNone (events.js:67:13)
    at TLSSocket.emit (events.js:166:7)
    at TLSSocket._finishInit (_tls_wrap.js:567:8)
LM-SJN-00712571:self-signed-cert jleblanc$ 
```

Figure 7-9. Error thrown when making POST requests with a self-signed certificate

Next we set up the HTTPS POST request object. We do this by using `https.request(…)`, passing in the `post_options` variable. In the response, we set the encoding of the response, then handle the case where data is sent back from the server with `res.on(…)`. In the case of our client, we are simply logging out the response.

Lastly, we send off the POST request to the server. If all went well, we should see the response shown in Figure 7-10 when using our client.

```
LM-SJN-00712571:self-signed-cert jleblanc$ node client.js
Message received:message=My%20secure%20JSON%20string
```

Figure 7-10. Response from HTTPS POST request

Asyncronous Cryptography

Asyncronous cryptography, also known as *public/private key encryption*, uses sets of public/private key pairs. A sender encrypts and signs, then a receiver decrypts and verifies any message that should be transmitted securely over a potentially insecure channel, such as when SSL is not available.

Some of these use cases may include multiuser environments over Internet-enabled hardware, small-scale microelectronics, or in any case where you might not be able to ensure the integrity of the connection for users.

What we have to know beforehand is how we will be working with these key sets (public/private keys) in order to secure the message being sent. The public-key part of the set can be known to anyone needing it (much like a username), while the private key must remain known only to the party it belongs to (much like a password).

Use Case

Let's look at a practical scenario of when this will be valuable. Suppose you're walking around a store with your mobile phone, and the store uses a series of BLE (Bluetooth low energy) devices, also known as *beacons*, for in-aisle purchasing. The device allows a phone to connect to it, and then it connects to a web endpoint to process the message. In this case, the messages may be to check the users in with their account, or to pay for their goods through a store credit card or PayPal account. These BLE beacons themselves are not secure devices and can be modified by a malicious party. We want to ensure that when users are sending their login information, the beacon hasn't been modified to transmit that clear-text data to a malicious endpoint instead of the store endpoint.

This is where public/private keys come in. The person sending the message encrypts the message with the public key of the recipient (perhaps through a public keystore that verifies requests from the application asking for the public key), and then signs the message with his private key (in the case of the person walking around the store, this might be embedded within their store application). The encrypted and signed versions of the message are transmitted through the beacon, and on to the store API endpoint. That store API endpoint then decrypts the encrypted message with its private key (perhaps stored securely on its servers), and the signed version is verified using the public key of the sender (the person walking around the store).

We have now decrypted the message and verified its origins. In doing so, we've mitigated a number of potential attack vectors:

- A malicious party cannot simply watch cleartext traffic through the beacon and store any sensitive information going back and forth, because we encrypt the data end-to-end.

- A malicious party cannot send fake data through to the endpoint with hopes of gaining user account access, as the private key is known only to the user, and the message verification would fail without the public-key signing.

- A malicious party cannot force the beacon to push data to its own endpoints and expect any valid results. The data might arrive, but without a method of decrypting the data or checking its validity, the information would not be beneficial.

Let's break this down into a simple process, shown in Figure 7-11.

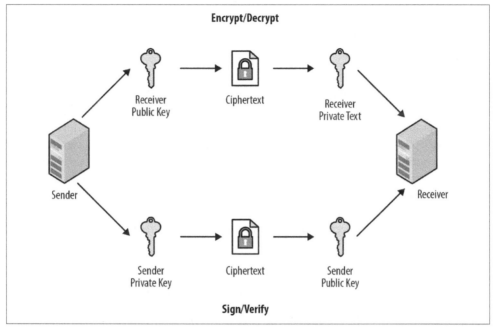

Figure 7-11. Asymmetric cryptography process

These are the steps that you follow as you transmit data:

1. You generate two sets of keys, public/private keys for the person sending the data (sender), and another public/private key set for the person receiving the data (receiver).

2. You create a small message (typically a string/JSON object or the like) that you would like to transmit.

3. From the sender side, you take that message and encrypt it with the receiver's public key, then take the encrypted message and sign it with your private key.

4. You transmit the encrypted and signed data to the recipient, sometimes through an intermediate device or service.

5. The recipient verifies the signed payload with the public key of the sender, then (if valid) decrypts the encrypted message with their private key.

You now have a verified and decoded message that can be processed as needed.

Implementation Example

Let's see this functionality in practice through a Node implementation of this process. We're going to break this into a three-step process to explore the main features of the example:

- Steps 1a/1b: Generating your two sets of public/private keys. 1a covers doing so directly in code, with no storage of the keys, while 1b takes that concept a bit further and shows you how to implement file storage for the public/private keys on top of that. For a proof of concept, 1a is an expedient way to get started, but for all production implementations, 1b is preferred. Choose one of these implementations as you are running through the examples.

- Step 2: Encrypting and signing a piece of data from the side of the sender, to be sent through to the receiver.

- Step 3: Decrypting and verifying the data that was sent from a sender.

When Keys Should Be Generated and Used

Even though we are showing a full end-to-end example that can be executed in a single pass, the code execution most likely shouldn't be structured this way in a production environment. If you have a sender/receiver relationship, typically the sender device will be registered with the receiver's service. When that device/site registration occurs, the public/private keys for that pairing (steps 1a or 1b) should be run. Only when the user begins using the service to transmit data (steps 2 and 3) should those keys then be extracted and used.

Let's start out with generating keys.

Step 1a: Generating keys without file storage

The complete sample code for the asymmetric key cryptography process without using the filesystem is available at *https://github.com/iddatasecuritybook/chapter7/blob/master/asymmetric-crypto/crypto_no_fs.js*.

The first thing we need to do when generating our needed public/private key pairs is to add in a Node package to help us with generating, encrypting, decrypting, signing, and verifying our keys.

There is a popular package, named `ursa`, for doing just that, and we install it like so:

```
npm install fs --save
```

Next, we add that package as a requirement at the top of our Node script:

```
var ursa = require('ursa');
```

Now that we have our packages defined, it's time to generate a few public and private keys that we are going to need during the process. As mentioned earlier, in this example we are going to simply generate these into variables without any file storage component:

```
//generate sender private and public keys
var senderKey = ursa.generatePrivateKey(1024, 65537);
var senderPrivKey = ursa.createPrivateKey(senderKey.toPrivatePem());
var senderPubKey = ursa.createPublicKey(senderKey.toPublicPem());

//generate recipient private and public keys
var recipientKey = ursa.generatePrivateKey(1024, 65537);
var recipientPrivKey = ursa.createPrivateKey(recipientKey.toPrivatePem());
var recipientPubKey = ursa.createPublicKey(recipientKey.toPublicPem());
```

In this code snippet, we are running the same three lines of code to generate keys for the sender and recipient.

When generating keys, the first item on our list is to make a request to the `ursa` `generatePrivateKey(...)` method, which will produce a random key set used to extract our individual public and private key pairs.

The parameters passed to `generatePrivateKey()` are as follows:

- The number of bits in the modulus (in the preceding case, 1024). Anything 1024 or over is generally considered secure, but the method defaults to 2048 if no number is specified.
- The exponent value, which must be odd. This argument is optional as well, and defaults to 65537.

We then need to break those up into our individual matching keys, using the `ursa` methods `createPrivateKey(…)` and `createPublicKey(…)`, which will accept our previously generated key set in the previous line as a parameter.

That parameter can be passed through as `senderkey.toPrivatePem()` or `sender key.toPublicPem()`, depending on whether you're attempting to generate a public or private key.

Next, let's look at doing the same thing, but this time using file storage for the keys.

Step 1b: Generating keys with file storage

The complete sample code for the asymmetric key cryptography process using the filesystem is available at *https://github.com/iddata securitybook/chapter7/blob/master/asymmetric-crypto/crypto_fs.js*.

Now, let's look at more of a production-level deployment, where we might be working with thousands of key pairs stored in a keystore, or having individual sender keys deployed through an application on a user's device.

As in the previous example, we'll include the `ursa` package for working with our public/private key pairs, but in addition to those we'll include a few others: `fs` for generating files and storing information on the filesystem, `path` for normalizing folder/file paths, and `mkdirp` for generating folder structures with some good duplicate folder handling without producing errors.

The `fs` and `path` packages are part of the core modules, so we don't need to define those. For the other two, we install them from npm like so:

```
npm install ursa --save
npm install mkdirp --save
```

As we have done many times before, we now add those packages as requirements to the top of our Node script:

```
var fs = require('fs');
var ursa = require('ursa');
var path = require('path');
var mkdirp = require('mkdirp');
```

We're going to streamline our key generation a bit, and instead of duplicating the code for generating just two sets of keys, we'll put that all together into a single public/private key generation function that we can call:

```
function makeKeys(rootPath, subPath){
    try {
        mkdirp.sync(path.join(rootPath, subPath));
    } catch (err) {
        console.error(err);
    }

    var key = ursa.generatePrivateKey(1024, 65537);
    var privatePem = key.toPrivatePem();
    var publicPem = key.toPublicPem();

    try {
        fs.writeFileSync(path.join(rootPath, subPath, 'private.pem'),
            privatePem, 'ascii');
```

```
        fs.writeFileSync(path.join(rootPath, subPath, 'public.pem'),
            publicPem, 'ascii');
    } catch (err) {
        console.error(err);
    }
}
```

Working with the Filesystem

Accessing the filesystem can be unreliable. Therefore, it's always a best practice to ensure that you are appropriately capturing and handling errors that are produced. A simplified example is displayed in the preceding code.

Our makekeys function will accept two parameters: a root path for where the keys will be stored (rootpath), and a subpath for separating out the public/private keys into individual folders (subpath). In the end, we are looking for a folder structure that looks something like this:

- *./keys/sender* (which includes the public/private *.pem* files for the sender)
- *./keys/receiver* (which includes the public/private *.pem* files for the sender)

We start by creating our necessary folder path with mkdirp.sync() for the path supplied. The path package will normalize the root and subpaths together for the folder locations to be created.

Working with mkdirp

Instead of producing errors when attempting to create a duplicate folder structure, mkdirp just continues with the next line of code execution. This makes mkdirp nice to work with in an environment in which someone could try to create a duplicate folder structure.

Over the next three lines, we use the ursa package to generate our key pairs, then extract the public and private keys into individual variables.

Lastly, we use the fs.writeFileSync(…) method to create our *.pem* files to hold the public and private keys. writeFile(…) in the preceding example will accept three parameters:

- The path and filename to write. In this case, it's our root and subfolders, with either *private.pem* or *public.pem* as the filename.
- The content to write, which is obtained from our variables holding the public and private keys.

- The content type, in this case ASCII.

Now that we have our function in place to create a public and private key where we designate, we can create both the key pairs for the sender and receiver with the following three lines:

```
var rootPath = './keys';
makeKeys(rootPath, 'sender');
makeKeys(rootPath, 'receiver');
```

We should now have the directory structure and four *.pem* files created. In a more realistic deployment, the content of these *.pem* files might be stored in a properly secured key storage lookup, or public keys separated into a public keystore that allows the lookup of keys for encryption or verification from verified sources, such as from application locations that were registered with the service.

Key Storage File Types

Numerous file-extension standards are used for public/private key storage, including (but definitely not limited to) *.pem* (can be used for the public key or for the entire public/private chain), *.key* (for just the private key), *.pub* (for just the public key), *.cert* (a *.pem* file with a different file extension that is recognized by Windows Explorer), as well as many others. Choose the one that works best for you. For more discussion on this topic, see this Server Fault exchange (*http://serverfault.com/questions/9708/what-is-a-pem-file-and-how-does-it-differ-from-other-openssl-generated-key-file/9717#9717*).

Now that we have our keys in place, we can follow the same type of methodology as we did in step 1a, but this time we're going to extract the contents of the keys from the *.pem* files we just wrote:

```
var rootPath = './keys';

//generate sender private and public keys
var senderPubKey = ursa.createPrivateKey(
    fs.readFileSync(path.join(rootPath, 'sender', 'private.pem')));
var senderpubkey = ursa.createPublicKey(
    fs.readFileSync(path.join(rootPath, 'sender', 'public.pem')));

//generate recipient private and public keys
var recipientPrivKey = ursa.createPrivateKey(
    fs.readFileSync(path.join(rootPath, 'receiver', 'private.pem')));
var recipientPubKey = ursa.createPublicKey(
    fs.readFileSync(path.join(rootPath, 'receiver', 'public.pem')));
```

We start with a given root path (same as when we generated the keys) that we should pull the keys from. For each key, we use the ursa package to create either a public or a private key. Because it is expecting the key content from the files we wrote, we use the `fs.readFileSync(...)` method to pull the content in, passing along the full path to our *.pem* files. In a full production deployment, these files would reference back to your particular keystore, where the *.pem* files are stored.

Next, we're going to see how to use these keys to encrypt and sign a message to be sent.

Step 2: Encrypting and signing a message

We're now at the stage where the user (the sender) is ready to send some data through a potentially insecure device or third party, on the way to the receiver. To prepare this data to be sent, we need to encrypt and sign it by using the keys that we just created:

```
//prepare JSON message to send
var msg = { 'user':'Nikola Tesla',
            'address':'W 40th St, New York, NY 10018',
            'state':'active' };

msg = JSON.stringify(msg);

//encrypt with recipient public key, and sign with sender private key
var encrypted = recipientPubKey.encrypt(msg, 'utf8', 'base64');
var signed = senderPrivKey.hashAndSign('sha256', encrypted, 'utf8', 'base64');
```

Let's say that the data that we are trying to send is a JSON structure with some privileged information, the `msg` variable in the code. To start out, let's go ahead and convert that into a string to be encrypted.

Next we use the recipient's public key (most likely obtained from a public keystore) to encrypt the data by calling `recipientPubKey.encrypt(...)`, passing in the string to be encrypted.

After we encrypt, we need to create a signed version of the encrypted data by using the sender's private key to hash and sign the encrypted string that we just created, which we do by calling `senderPrivKey.hashAndSign(...)`, passing in the hashing algorithm (SHA-256) and the encrypted string.

We now have two variables: the encrypted version and the signed version. We take those two variables and transmit them through the third-party device or service.

Let's say the device working as the transmitter between the sender and the receiver is compromised. Without the private key of the recipient, the raw JSON structure can't be extracted. In essence, if the data is sniffed, it will be completely useless.

We're now at the stage where the data has transferred through the third-party device or service, and has arrived safely at the recipient for decryption and verification.

Step 3: Decrypting and signing a message

With the data safely in the hands of the recipient, we need to both extract the data and ensure that the data is coming from a valid source through our matching public/private key pairs:

```
//verify message with sender private key
var bufferedMsg = new Buffer(encrypted);
if (!senderPubKey.hashAndVerify('sha256', bufferedMsg, signed, 'base64')) {
    throw new Error("invalid signature");
} else {
    //decrypt message with recipient private key
    var decryptedMsg = recipientPrivKey.decrypt(encrypted, 'base64', 'utf8');
    console.log('decrypted message verified:', decryptedMsg);
}
```

We start out by verifying the data that was sent over, to ensure that the originally signed data is from the source that we expect it to be. We create a buffer out of the encrypted message, for comparison. We then use senderPubKey.hashAndVerify(…), passing in the same hashing algorithm we used to sign the data, along with the buffer of our encrypted string, and the signed version of the data that we received from the sender. What is happening here is that we are comparing the encrypted ciphertext against the signed ciphertext that we received from the sender. If they don't match, we have an unverified data object; but if they match, we have valid data and can then move to decrypt the data packet.

Once verified, we now decrypt the data that was transmitted over. As you may recall, we originally encrypted the data with the recipient's public key, so now we can decrypt that data only by using the matching recipient private key by passing the encrypted message to recipientPrivKey.decrypt(…).

If we print that out, we'll see the original JSON structure that we started with. Now that we have a verified and decrypted message, we can begin using the data however we need to.

Advantages, Disadvantages, and Uses of Aynchronous Cryptography

Aynchronous, or public key, cryptography has advantages when compared against synchronous cryptography methods. In the same light, we also have to deal with a few drawbacks with this method.

Let's look at a few of the benefits here:

Key convenience
> Because each party (sender and receiver) has their own private key, and that key doesn't need to be transmitted, we don't have to deal with trying to find a secure method for transmitting that data as we do in a synchronous environment.

Key nonrepudiation

Because each party owns their own private key, and that value is never shared, an attack case involving a piece of data with an authenticated server but a potentially compromised key is a nonissue. Each party is responsible for the secure storage of their private keys, meaning that this issue doesn't come up.

Now, we are dealing with one pretty big negative when working with this method:

Speed

Because a lot of processing needs to happen during encryption and decryption when using this method, it is quite slow when compared to a synchronous model.

With all of this said, asynchronous cryptography is not overly well suited for a single-user environment, where you might be encrypting data to be sent between two parties that you own. This is where synchronous cryptography shines. This method works well in a multiuser environment, where the channels between a sender and receiver might not be secure.

Synchronous Cryptography

With asynchronous cryptography, we've explored the realms of transmitting data through potentially insecure channels. The use of public and private keys in our examples is similar to the methodology behind technologies such as OAuth and OpenID Connect.

Now that you have that understanding, let's see how to further protect data transmission between two sources that trust each other. Think of it this way: let's say I'm writing an email through my Gmail account to be sent to another Gmail account, Google is transmitting data through a secure HTTPS connection, and we can safely assume that the email at the end of the line is from an authentic source.

One of the main uses for synchronous cryptography is in a trusted environment. Instead of using two separate public and private keys, we instead use a shared secret between two sources. Using a single key can significantly increase the encryption and decryption speed, but at the same time, if the single key is compromised, the resulting damage might be worse.

At a high level, Figure 7-12 shows how this process works end-to-end with a single shared secret key.

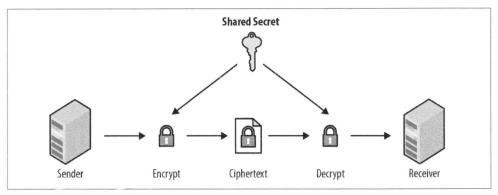

Figure 7-12. Symmetric cryptography process

In the image, we see that

- The sender has a piece of plain-text data that they intend to send to the receiver over the channel.
- The sender uses the shared secret to encrypt the data, giving us the ciphertext.
- When the receiver obtains the ciphertext, they use the same shared secret to decrypt the ciphertext into its original plain text.

Next, we'll run through a few practical examples of synchronous cryptography by using AES Block ciphering with a few different modes of operation using an initialization vector. Before we do that, though, let's see what initialization vectors and padding are, how these modes of operation differ, and how they affect the block cipher security and performance.

Initialization Vector

Many of the cryptographic algorithms that we are likely to use are what we call *iterative algorithms*. When a piece of data that is to be encrypted is split into blocks for encryption, those iterative algorithms depend on the data from previously encrypted blocks in order to process the next subsequent block. In these cases, the first block of data that will be encrypted has no previous block to build, so it needs a piece of data to begin running the algorithm. This is the initialization vector.

An *initialization vector* is a fixed-sized piece of data that is typically required to be random, or at the least, pseudorandom. Typically, each time you are encrypting a new piece of data, you would supply a new, random, fixed-length piece of data.

Let's look at a practical example. In the CBC encryption mode of operation (we will explore that in the next section), the way it works is by breaking the data to be encrypted into blocks. As the algorithm goes through each block, the plain-text block is XORed (*exclusive or*—A or B, but not A and B) against the previous encrypted block, before finally being encrypted together. Because the first block in the chain needs to have a previous block to XOR against, we need to supply that data. That data is the initialization vector.

Padding

In the case of certain block cipher algorithm modes, such as Cipher Block Chaining (CBC) described in the next section, when the data to be encrypted is split into blocks of data to be processed, the plain-text data that is to be encrypted needs to be an exact multiple of the blocks produced. This means that each block needs to be an equal size. In these cases, if we come across data that cannot be chunked up into equal blocks, we need to add some padding data to the blocks.

Several standard conventions are employed that set standards on what this dummy data should be. Let's look at these visually. Let's say that we want to encode the string "This is my block data." If the cipher mode we are employing requires equal block sizes, it would split the data into three blocks of 8 bytes, represented with the hex values of each character:

```
+---------------------+---------------------+---------------------+
|T  h  i  s  _  i  s  _|m  y  _  b  l  o  c  k|_  d  a  t  a  ?  ?  ?|
+---------------------+---------------------+---------------------+
|54 68 69 73 20 69 73 20|6d 79 20 62 6c 6f 63 6b|20 64 61 74 61 ?? ?? ??|
+---------------------+---------------------+---------------------+
```

Those three characters at the end will be the padding that we need to add to the string. Let's see how this looks with each convention:

Each padded byte is the value of the total number of bytes needing to be added
Each byte of padding is set to the value of the total number of bytes of padding. In this case, we have 3 bytes of padding, so we set the value to 03:

```
+---------------------+---------------------+---------------------+
|T  h  i  s  _  i  s  _|m  y  _  b  l  o  c  k|_  d  a  t  a  _  _  _|
+---------------------+---------------------+---------------------+
|54 68 69 73 20 69 73 20|6d 79 20 62 6c 6f 63 6b|20 64 61 74 61 03 03 03|
+---------------------+---------------------+---------------------+
```

 The preceding convention is the most popular method used throughout the industry, as it's easy during decryption to read these padding bytes and know, easily, what is a padding byte and how many you should be looking for.

The first padded byte is 0x80, followed by 0 bytes for the rest

For this one, we set the first byte of padding to 0x80 and all subsequent padding bytes to 0:

```
+-----------------------+-----------------------+-----------------------+
|T  h  i  s  _  i  s  _ |m  y  _  b  l  o  c  k |_  d  a  t  a  _  _  _ |
+-----------------------+-----------------------+-----------------------+
|54 68 69 73 20 69 73 20|6d 79 20 62 6c 6f 63 6b|20 64 61 74 61 80 00 00|
+-----------------------+-----------------------+-----------------------+
```

Each byte is set to 0 except the last byte, which is the number of the total bytes of padding

This is a take on the first method, but we set all bytes of padding to 0, with the exception of the last byte, which should be equal to the total number of bytes of padding. In the case of our example, that will be 03:

```
+-----------------------+-----------------------+-----------------------+
|T  h  i  s  _  i  s  _ |m  y  _  b  l  o  c  k |_  d  a  t  a  _  _  _ |
+-----------------------+-----------------------+-----------------------+
|54 68 69 73 20 69 73 20|6d 79 20 62 6c 6f 63 6b|20 64 61 74 61 00 00 03|
+-----------------------+-----------------------+-----------------------+
```

All bytes are set to 0

All bytes of padding should be set to 0:

```
+-----------------------+-----------------------+-----------------------+
|T  h  i  s  _  i  s  _ |m  y  _  b  l  o  c  k |_  d  a  t  a  _  _  _ |
+-----------------------+-----------------------+-----------------------+
|54 68 69 73 20 69 73 20|6d 79 20 62 6c 6f 63 6b|20 64 61 74 61 00 00 00|
+-----------------------+-----------------------+-----------------------+
```

All bytes are set to spaces (0x20)

All bytes of padding should be set to spaces:

```
+-----------------------+-----------------------+-----------------------+
|T  h  i  s  _  i  s  _ |m  y  _  b  l  o  c  k |_  d  a  t  a  _  _  _ |
+-----------------------+-----------------------+-----------------------+
|54 68 69 73 20 69 73 20|6d 79 20 62 6c 6f 63 6b|20 64 61 74 61 20 20 20|
+-----------------------+-----------------------+-----------------------+
```

How padding works is something that we should understand when choosing a proper mode of operation, because it can be costly depending on the data that is to be encrypted. In each case of the padding, the decryption process needs to know how to properly determine which method was used, and how to properly disregard padding values.

In the case of the algorithms that we are going to use in the practical examples that follow, padding will be taken care of for us, so it's not something that we need to be concerned with in our implementations.

Block Cipher Modes of Operation

Understanding the potential modes of operation is important when working with data encryption. A *mode of operation* is an algorithm that uses a block cipher (such as AES) to provide functionality such as confidentiality or data authentication for the block of information to be encrypted.

Within the case of our web operations, we will be working with three main categories of modes:

Encryption
> This means, in general terms, data privacy/confidentiality. A potential attacker who has the generated ciphertext (the encrypted data) will not be able to get any information about the plain-text data, except for the length perhaps.

Authentication
> Authentication mode provides a mechanism for determining data authenticity. If a receiver obtains ciphertext or cleartext from a sender, they can determine whether the data is genuine and was constructed by the sender.

Authenticated Encryption
> This includes both previous categories.

Now that we have an understanding of the categories, let's look at some of the NIST-approved block cipher modes of operation[1] (Table 7-1). Many of these modes range heavily in how they function, but at the end of this section we list the most popular industry-standard modes.

Table 7-1. Encryption modes of operation

Mode	Name	Description
ECB	Electronic Codebook	The simplest mode of operation. The data that is supplied for encryption is divided into blocks. When encrypting/decrypting, these blocks are processed individually. The main issue with this mode is that identical plain-text blocks are encrypted into identical ciphertext blocks, which creates a pattern that a potential hacker can exploit. One of the benefits of this mode is that the blocks can be processed in parallel, speeding up encryption/decryption.
CBC	Cipher Block Chaining	In this mode, each plain-text block is XORed against the previous ciphertext (encrypted) block, before then being encrypted itself. Since this is an iterative algorithm, an initialization vector needs to be supplied. In order to make each block unique, the initialization vector needs to be supplied as the first block. One of the chief drawbacks is that blocks cannot be processed in parallel, since each block needs to be run sequentially. The other issue is that plain-text input needs to be a multiple of the block size (each block the same size), meaning that the initial data may have to be padded to bring it to that length.

---

1 *http://csrc.nist.gov/groups/ST/toolkit/BCM/index.html*

Mode	Name	Description
OFB	Output Feedback	The output of OFB is what is called a stream cipher. The plain-text blocks are combined with random or pseudorandom characters to generate keystream blocks. These keystream blocks are then XORed with the plain-text blocks to get the end ciphertext. This mode also utilizes a supplied intialization vector. One of the benefits with this mode is that each block can be a different size, meaning that there is no need to pad the initial plain-text data. One of the drawbacks is that encrypting and decrypting blocks cannot be done in parallel, since encrypting each block depends on the previous blocks.
CFB	Cipher Feedback	CFB mode is very similar operationally to CBC. The main difference between these two is that CBC mode creates the ciphertext after the block cipher algorithm is run, while CFB generates it after we compute the XOR.
CTR	Counter	Counter mode, much like OFB, turns the block cipher into a stream cipher. The keystream that is used can be a function that produces successive values for the random data (a counter). The function producing the counter data just needs to ensure that the data does not repeat for a long period of time. The most common counter type is one that increments a number by 1 each time. Where CTR differs from OFB is that both CTR encryption and decryption can be run in parallel, since it doesn't generate the ciphertext by XORing the plain-text block against the previous ciphertext block (as in OFB).

If you want to protect the privacy of the data that you are sending, but don't necessarily need to authenticate the sending source of the data, then the mode under the encryption category will fill that need.

If confidentiality is not required for the message being sent, that's where the authentication mode will come into play. For instance, if you just need to know that the message came from an approved sender, but the message itself is not sensitive in terms of data privacy, then the mode of operation in Table 7-2 is probably best.

Table 7-2. Authentication modes of operation

Mode	Name	Description
CMAC	Cipher-based Message Authentication Code	CMAC mode is used for determining the authenticity and integrity of a message. It uses a block cipher algorithm in conjunction with a secret key to generate the resulting cipher. This mode is not heavily used.

In many cases you probably want to not only maintain the privacy of the data being transmitted, but also verify the source of the data for additional security. In this case, the combined authenticated encryption modes listed in Table 7-3 are an excellent option.

Table 7-3. Authenticated encryption modes of operation

Mode	Name	Description
CCM	Counter with CBC-MAC	This is the easiest combined mode of operation. As the full name suggests, CCM is a combination of the CTR and CBC modes of operation. This mode also includes the use of an initialization vector, and message authentication is done on the plain-text data. Encryption/decryption cannot be run in parallel.

Mode	Name	Description
GCM	Galois/Counter Mode	GCM has been widely adopted because of its efficiency and performance. Like CCM, GCM uses an initialization vector, but the message authentication is done on the ciphertext as opposed to the plain-text data. Encryption/decryption can also be run in parallel, unlike CCM.
KW / KWP / TKW	Key Wrapping	Permutations of proposed key wrap algorithm modes for encrypting and authenticating data. These modes are not widely used.

Even with a basic understanding of the preceding tables, it can be difficult to choose the best modes of operations in each category. If we break them into current industry-standard use, these are the most popular modes of operation in each category:

- Encryption: CTR (for good parallelization/speed)
- Authentication: CMAC (because it's the only approved one, although it's not widely used in the industry)
- Authenticated Encryption: GCM (industry-accepted standard)

Even though there are preferred modes by many in the industry, the mode that you choose to use should always come down to your needs on security, performance, scaling, and how each mode fits into those plans. Just because it's popular doesn't mean it's right for you.

Now that you have an understanding of modes of operation, let's apply these to a few examples, starting with AES using the CTR encryption mode.

Using AES with CTR Encryption Mode

This sample code for using AES with CTR mode is available at *https://github.com/iddatasecuritybook/chapter7/blob/master/ symmetric-crypto/aes-ctr.js*.

We have all the our core basics to start looking at using a cipher algorithm (AES) with a particular mode of operation (CTR encryption in this case).

We're going to be using the standard Node crypto package (*https://nodejs.org/api/ crypto.html*) for this example, so there is nothing to pull down from npm. At the top of your Node script, add the following initialization variable:

```
var crypto = require('crypto');
```

Now we need to set the variables that we are going to be working with in the example:

```
var text = "Encryption Testing AES";
var key = crypto.randomBytes(32);        //256 bit shared key
var iv = crypto.randomBytes(16);         //initialization vector - 16 bytes
var algorithm = 'aes-256-ctr';           //cipher and mode of operation
```

Going from top to bottom, these are as follows:

text
> The data to be encrypted/decrypted.

key
> A 32-byte shared key to be used by the crypto library for encryption/decryption. We use the `crypto.randomBytes(…)` method to generate that string.

iv
> The initialization vector, which should be a random 16-byte string. We use the `crypto.randomBytes(…)` method to generate that string.

algorithm
> The cipher algorithm and mode of operation to use. In this case, we're using the AES cipher algorithm with the CTR mode of operation.

Next, we create the ciphertext by encrypting the data:

```
var cipher = crypto.createCipher(algorithm, key, iv);
var encrypted = cipher.update(text, 'utf8', 'hex');
encrypted += cipher.final('hex');
```

We first make a call to `crypto.createCipher(…)` to initialize the cipher that we want to use, passing in the algorithm/mode, the shared key, and the initialization vector.

Next, we use `cipher.update(…)` to update the cipher with data. We supply the data to be encoded, the input encoding utf8, and the output encoding hex.

cipher.update(data, input_encoding, output_encoding)

The input encoding (second parameter) should be one of utf8, ascii, or binary. If no input encoding is specified, the data (first parameter) must be a Buffer. If a Buffer is specified as the data, input encoding will be ignored.

Lastly, we make the request to `cipher.final(…)`, passing in the output encoding type, to return the ciphertext.

Our plain-text input is now encoded. At this point, there should be a few things known about the ciphertext and decryption:

- The ciphertext can now be transmitted to its end source (the receiver).
- The shared key and initialization vector must be known to the receiver to decrypt. The key should be a shared secret between the app and the host (sender and receiver), and the IV can be considered as a one-time-use nonce, shared between both parties.

Now, let's say the cipher has been transmitted to the receiver, and they also have the key and initialization vector. We can now begin deciphering the ciphertext to extract our plain-text message:

```
var decipher = crypto.createDecipher(algorithm, key, iv);
var decrypted = decipher.update(encrypted, 'hex', 'utf8');
decrypted += decipher.final('utf8');
```

We start by making a call to `crypto.createDecipher(…)`, passing along the same values that we did for creating the cipher during encryption.

We then call `decipher.update(…)`, passing in the ciphertext, the ciphertext encoding (in this case, `hex`), and the intended output encoding (in this case, `utf8`).

Lastly, we call `decipher.final(…)` with the output encoding type to retrieve our final decoded message.

Using AES with with GCM Authenticated Encryption Mode

 This sample code for using AES with GCM mode is available at *https://github.com/iddatasecuritybook/chapter7/blob/master/ symmetric-crypto/aes-gcm.js.*

Now let's look at an example that uses the GCM joint authenticated encryption mode of operation. This one is fairly similar to the previous CTR mode example, but with an additional encryption/decryption step to handle the authentication piece that we didn't have in the CTR mode example.

We're again going to use the standard Node crypto package, so require that at the top of your Node script:

```
var crypto = require('crypto');
```

Next, we initialize the variables that we are going to be using:

```
var text = "Encryption Testing AES GCM mode";
var key = crypto.randomBytes(32);       //256 bit shared key
var iv = crypto.randomBytes(16);        //initialization vector - 16 bytes
var algorithm = 'aes-256-gcm';          //cipher and mode of operation
```

As before, these variables are as follows:

text

>The data to be encrypted/decrypted.

key

>A 32-byte shared key to be used by the crypto library for encryption/decryption. We use the `crypto.randomBytes(…)` method to generate that string.

iv

>The initialization vector, which should be a random 16-byte string. We use the `crypto.randomBytes(…)` method to generate that string.

algorithm

>The cipher algorithm and mode of operation to use. In this case, we're using the AES cipher algorithm with the GCM authenticated encryption mode of operation.

Now, let's encode the data to get our ciphertext, and see the differences when we add the authentication piece:

```
var cipher = crypto.createCipher(algorithm, key, iv);
var encrypted = cipher.update(text, 'utf8', 'hex');
encrypted += cipher.final('hex');
var tag = cipher.getAuthTag();
```

We first make a call to `crypto.createCipher(…)` to initialize the cipher, passing in the algorithm/mode, the shared key, and the initialization vector.

Next, we use `cipher.update(…)` to update the cipher with data. We supply the data to be encoded, the input encoding utf8, and the output encoding hex.

We then create the ciphertext by calling `cipher.final(…)` with the output formatting.

This is where the authentication piece comes in; after we have the ciphertext, we have to generate a tag by calling `cipher.getAuthTag(…)`. This will be a Buffer containing an authentication tag that has been computed from the cipher data. This will be used to authenticate the source of the ciphertext.

As of the writing of this text, `getAuthTag` supports only the GCM authenticated encryption mode.

As in the previous example, the ciphertext should be transmitted to the receiver. The receiver should also have knowledge of the shared key, the initialization vector, and the authentication tag:

```
var decipher = crypto.createDecipher(algorithm, key, iv);
decipher.setAuthTag(tag);
var decrypted = decipher.update(encrypted, 'hex', 'utf8');
decrypted += decipher.final('utf8');
```

We make our call to `crypto.createDecipher(…)`, passing along the same values that we did for creating the cipher during encryption.

Following that, we need to pass in the authentication tag to validate the source of the ciphertext. We do so by calling `decipher.setAuthTag(…)`, passing in the tag that was generated from the encryption step.

Next, we go back to the standard decipher techniques by calling `decipher.update(…)` to pass in the data, providing the ciphertext, ciphertext encoding (in this case, `hex`), and the intended output encoding (in this case, `utf8`).

Lastly, we call `decipher.final(…)` with the output encoding type to retrieve our final decoded message. The ciphertext will now be decoded and the source authenticated, allowing us to use the data at will.

Advantages, Disadvantages, and Uses of Synchronous Cryptography

As we close out our exploration of synchronous cryptography, it's a good idea to understand what it does well, and what it doesn't do well.

Using this method over its asymmetric counterpart has some advantages:

Security
> When we are using a secure algorithm, such as the US government–designated Advanced Encryption Standard (AES) that we looked at previously, the ciphertext that is produced is incredibly secure, and is considered essentially unbreakable with current computing standards.

Speed
> One of the main issues with asymmetric key cryptography is the complexity of the process that it needs for encryption and decryption. With symmetric cryptography, using modes of operation that allow for parallel block processing for encryption and decryption, we have a fast processing mechanism.

If we flip the coin, though, this methodology has one major drawback:

Shared key

As you saw in the practical examples, we generate a single shared key that is used by the sender for encryption, as well as the receiver for decryption. You need to take great care in ensuring that this key can be shared between both parties, without being retrieved by an attacker. Should this key be obtained by an illicit third party, they now have access to all encrypted data that is using that shared key. This means that the amount of damage that may be caused by using this method is typically quite high.

With all said and done, one of the best methods for using this type of cryptography is when you're encrypting and decrypting your own data, when you have safe, secure access to shared keys between endpoints. All in all, if you have a safe way to share the key between yourself and an unknown party, you probably don't need to be using your own encryption in the first place.

GitHub Repositories

We are well aware that mistakes might have slipped into the code that were not spotted throughout the review period, that code needs to be updated in order to reflect current trends, or that those libraries and modules we build upon are deprecated in favor of something better. This is why we have created an organization on GitHub (*http://github.com/iddatasecuritybook*) that holds all code we present throughout this book. You will find the complete OAuth 2 and OpenID Connect server, the client that interacts with those service providers, and all those small snippets we use to demonstrate certain features.

If you have any questions or want to contribute, please feel free to create an issue on GitHub or fork the affected project, make the change, and send us a pull request. We promise to proactively improve the code over time in order to ensure longevity of the information we conveyed here.

Technical Preconditions and Requirements

This appendix explains some basic concepts around Node and adds extra material that supplements the book's content.

On ES6/ES2015

You'll notice that we are using ES5 syntax as a base for the code throughout this book. The simple reason is that we wanted to use the more common syntax to ensure that everyone is able to comfortably read through this book.

We highly encourage you to try out ES6 by using compilers/transpilers such as Babel (*http://babeljs.io/docs/usage/cli*). Node is slowly adopting ES6—in the meantime, you can prepare your application and ensure that you are ready to deploy to production when ES6 is fully supported.

Setting Up Your Node.js Environment

This book assumes a working Node.js environment and the ability to install various modules using npm. This section runs through setting up Node in order to ensure that you will be able to follow the book.

First, install Node by either downloading and running the installer from nodejs.org's Downloads section (*http://nodejs.org/en/download*) or leveraging a package manager such as brew (*http://blog.teamtreehouse.com/install-node-js-npm-mac*), pacman, or apt-get (*http://nodejs.org/en/download/package-manager*). Verify that the installation worked by typing `which node` or `node -v` into your terminal—this should display either the path to your node executable or your local node version.

The download from nodejs.org always serves the most recent stable version of Node and should be favored over alternative ways of installing Node whenever possible.

Once Node is set up, you can proceed with installing Express by utilizing npm. To see if your environment is working correctly, simply enter npm in your terminal. You should see a brief explanation about using the command.

Managing Node Versions or Alternative Installations

By using the installer obtained from nodejs.org, the newest stable version of Node.js will be installed on your machine. Sometimes you might have to use another version of Node or even switch between multiple versions based on the project you are working on. nvm (which stands for Node Version Manager) is a community project that allows for doing exactly this.

You can use the install script for cURL by running the following command:

```
curl -o- https://raw.githubusercontent.com/creationix/nvm/v0.31.0/install.sh | bash
```

Assuming you'd like to install version 5.7.0 of Node.js (the latest stable version of Node), you'd run the following command:

```
nvm install 5.7.0
```

Once the installation is done, run nvm use 5.7.0 and your environment is set up: 5.7.0 will be your system's default Node.js version.

Should you be required to run multiple versions of Node, you have the choice of running the specific version either by using the command-line interface nvm run 5.7.0 or by setting up a project-specific .nvmrc file containing the target version number.

Installing the Express Generator

Assuming the setup works as intended, you can proceed by installing and using the Express generator. This generator allows for scaffolding your project and creating a reasonable structure:

```
npm install -g express-generator
```

You will notice that we use the -g option. This implies that we want to install the generator globally and not just as a module for our current project.

To verify that the Express generator was set up correctly, type the following command to see the generator's usage information:

```
express --help
```

You can find more documentation on the generator and Express on ExpressJS.com (*http://expressjs.com/en/starter/generator.html*).

Setting Up Express

If you'd like to avoid using a generator to set up your first Express project, you can start by following these instructions:

1. Create a new folder with `mkdir projectname`.

2. Navigate to the folder by running `cd projectname`.

3. Create a *package.json* file by running `npm init` in your project's root folder. Don't worry about fleshing out the content yet—the next section will go into *package.json* in more detail.

4. Run *touch app.js* (or whatever name you defined in step 3) to create your application's entry point. Here you'll define many of the modules your project ends up using, create the server itself, and initialize the middleware your project might rely on (see Chapter 4).

5. Finally, run `npm install express --save` to install the most important module for your project: Express itself.

After you've taken care of these five steps you're ready to implement a basic Express application that you can then build out in order to achieve additional functionality:

```
var app = require('express')();

app.get('/', function(req, res) {
  res.send('Hello from Express!');
});

app.listen(3000, function() {
  console.log('App active on port 3000');
});
```

The preceding example presents the beauty of Express: with a mere nine lines of code, you can run a simple web server. By navigating to `localhost:3000`, you'll be presented with a hearty `Hello from Express!`.

Run the application with the following command: `node app.js`. Congratulations!

You can extend this by starting to serve static resources (such as your site's CSS and JavaScript or images) by modifying the preceding example:

```
var express = require('express');
var app = express();

app.use(express.static('public'));
```

```
app.get('/', function(req, res) {
  res.send('Hello from Express!');
});

app.listen(3000, function() {
  console.log('App active on port 3000');
});
```

You can also specify that static resources are served through another folder structure such as */resources* by using the following method:

```
app.use('/resources', express.static('public'));
```

It is safer to declare the folder by using the absolute path to the folder: __dirname + '/public'. express.static uses relative paths—this leads to issues when running the Node process from another folder:

```
app.use('/static', express.static(__dirname + '/public'));
```

Creating and Maintaining Your package.json File

If you've been using the Express generator, you will notice that a file called *package.json* was generated for you. Otherwise, go ahead and create one by running npm init in your terminal.

package.json contains information about module dependencies, the project's authors, versioning, and a section called scripts containing commands for npm. In the following example case, running npm start or npm run start starts a new instance of your newly generated Node server:

```
{
  "name": "book",
  "version": "1.0.0",
  "private": true,
  "scripts": {
    "start": "node ./bin/www"
  },
  "dependencies": {
    "body-parser": "~1.13.2",
    "cookie-parser": "~1.3.5",
    "debug": "~2.2.0",
    "express": "~4.13.1",
    "jade": "~1.11.0",
    "morgan": "~1.6.1",
    "serve-favicon": "~2.3.0"
  }
}
```

You can also extend the `scripts` section for other tasks, like running `eslint`:

```
"scripts": {
  "start": "node ./bin/www",
  "lint": "eslint app.js lib/** routes/**"
},
...
```

Damon Bauer wrote a great blog post on using npm scripts for a variety of tasks that normally would be covered through task runners like grunt, gulp, or broccoli.[1] It's a highly recommended read in case you are looking for further inspiration.

By running `npm install`, all entries in the `dependencies` section will be retrieved. `npm update --save` ensures that your project uses the latest version of each dependency in the `dependencies` section and updates *package.json* accordingly. The site *http://www.npmjs.com* allows you to search for modules or browse popular choices—you will notice that `npm` itself is a module that can be updated using `npm`.

Additional sections—such as `bugs`—can be defined to help developers understand how to interact best with the project, how to contact the developers in case they want to get in touch, or under which license the project was published. Check out *http://browsenpm.org/package.json* for an interactive overview about all possible *package.json* sections.

Application Configuration

Environment variables are a sensible way of handling configuration details, such as database passwords or third-party API credentials, without hardcoding them in your application's code. The Twelve-Factor App methodology (*http://12factor.net/config*) defines this as separation of code and configuration and sees the benefit of being able to quickly change between different deployment targets such as production environments.

The module `dotenv` (*http://github.com/motdotla/dotenv*) was designed to specifically cater to this use case and utilizes a configuration file called *.env* (located in your project's root folder) that stores information in the `NAME=VALUE` format:

```
MONGO_DB=mongodb://localhost/database
MONGO_USER=tim
MONGO_PW=sloths-are-more-awesome-than-monkeys
```

---

1 *http://css-tricks.com/why-npm-scripts*

You can access these details by loading the module and calling the `config` method. You will notice that *process.env* is going to be populated with the information from your *.env* file:

```
require('dotenv').config();

var mongoose = require('mongoose');
mongoose.connect(process.env.MONGO_DB);
```

dotenv allows you to pass configuration options, such as `path` (in case you require a different location for your configuration file), `silent` (which suppresses warnings when no *.env* file can be found), or `encoding` (the default is `utf8`).

Version Control and Configuration Files

Make sure to exclude your `dotenv` configuration files by adding them to your project's *.gitignore* file. Please also check out the dotenv FAQ for more information on this matter.[2]

Working with JSON/URL-Encoded Bodies in Express

As of Express 4.0, working with JSON- and URL-encoded bodies has changed slightly, and requires an additional setup step to be able to work with that data when it is POSTed to your server. The `body-parser` npm module, when used in the following format, will allow your server to support those entities:

```
var bodyParser = require('body-parser')
var app = require('express')();
app.use(bodyParser.json());
app.use(bodyParser.urlencoded({
    extended: true
}));
```

---

2 *http://github.com/motdotla/dotenv#should-i-commit-my-env-file*

Glossary

2FA / Two-factor authentication

The process of using a secondary means of identification during a login or user discovery step. Typically, your first authentication system is a username and password, then your second factor of authentication may be a code provided by SMS to a registered phone number, a registered fingerprint, code via email, etc.

Ciphertext

Unreadable output of an encryption algorithm.

Cleartext

Human-readable data that is transmitted or stored unencrypted.

EFF

The Electronic Frontier Foundation. A nonprofit dedicated to protecting user privacy and civil liberties in the digital world.

Entropy

In the context of identity, this concerns the amount of information that is discoverable about users, determining the likelihood that users are who they say they are.

MFA

Multifactor authentication is a means of user identification that requires more than one method of authenication (username and password, SMS code, email code, fingerprint, etc.).

NIST

The National Institute of Standards and Technology, a unit of the US Commerce Department. NIST promotes and maintains measurement standards and maintains active programs for encouraging and assisting industry and science to develop and use these standards.

OWASP

The Open Web Application Security Project is a community that maintains tools, documentation, and guides in the field of web application security, and is considered a forefront standard in the space.

Plain text

Human-readable data that is supplied to the encryption algorithm

Security-layering

The practice of using multiple security mechanisms in a stacked approach to protect identity, data, and resources.

U2F

Universal 2nd Factor is an open authentication security standard that aims to strethen/simplify two-factor authentication using specialized USB or NFC devices based on similar security technology found in smart cards.

UAF

The Universal Authentication Framework protocol defines the process for password-less user experiences. This may be through voice commands, facial recognition, or another similar standard.

Index

Authy
    two-factor authentication with, 106-112
    when to delete users from, 111
    when to register new user with, 108
    when to send SMS verification code, 109
    when to validate verification code, 110

B
banks, face recognition software used by, 114
Basic Client flow, 97
bcrypt, 12, 36
Bearer Token, 65
biometrics, 112-115
    as username instead of password, 112
    face recognition, 114
    rating effectiveness of, 113-115
    retina/iris scanning, 114
    vein recognition, 115
Bitcoin, blockchain and, 118
bits of entropy, 48
BLE (Bluetooth low energy) devices, 149
block cipher modes of operation, 162-164
blockchain, 118
blowfish cypher, 36
Bluetooth devices, fingerprinting, 55
Bluetooth low energy (BLE) devices, 149
body-parser module, 144
browser fingerprinting, 47-52, 101
    capturing browser details, 50
    configurations more resistant to, 48
    identifiable browser information, 49
    JavaScript library for plug-in information,
        51
    plug-ins for, 51
    screen resolution, 51
    time zone, 51
    user agent, 50
brute force attacks, 20-22

C
CA (certificate authority), 138
CAPTCHA (Completely Automated Public
    Turing test to tell Computers and Humans
    Apart)
    creating with reCAPTCHA, 22-28
    limiting use of, 22
CBC (Cipher Block Chaining) encryption
    mode, 163

CCM (Counter with CBC-MAC) authenticated
    encryption mode, 163
certificate authority (CA), 138
certificate file (CRT), 143
certificate signing request (CSR), 142
certificate validation, 139-141
    domain validation, 139
    extended validation, 140
    organization validation, 139
    self-signed certificates, 141-148
CFB (Cypher Feedback) encryption mode, 163
Chrome, XSS Auditor with, 128
Cipher Block Chaining (CBC) encryption
    mode, 163
cipher.update(…), 165
Claims, 66
Client Credentials Grant, 96
client, OAuth 2.0, 92-96
    adding OpenID Connect functionality to,
        96-98
    custom URL schemes, 95
    OpenID Connect Basic flow, 97
    storing tokens on, 94
    using Authorization Codes, 92-95
client-side storage, cookies and, 120
CMAC (Cipher-based Message Authentication
    Code), 163
concrete identity, 44
configuration, 177
cookie-signature module, 124
cookies, 94, 120
Counter (CTR) encryption mode (see CTR
    encryption mode)
Counter with CBC-MAC (CCM) authenticated
    encryption mode, 163
cross-site request forgery (CSRF) attacks (see
    CSRF attacks)
cross-site scripting (XSS) (see XSS)
CRT (certificate) file, 143
crypto (Node package)
    for AES with CTR encryption, 164-166
    for AES with GCM authenticated encryp-
        tion, 166-168
    for random salt generation, 33
cryptography (see asynchronous cryptography)
    (see synchronous cryptography)
CSR (certificate signing request), 142
CSRF (cross-site request forgery) attacks, 68,
    130-132

UserInfo endpoint, 66
UserInfo endpoint modification, 91
organization validation (OV), 139
OTP (one-time passwords), 103-106
Output Feedback (OFB) encryption mode, 163
Oz, 117

P

package.json file, 176
padding, 160
palm vein recognition, 115
Panopticlick, 47, 101
password
  biometrics as alternative to, 112
  entropy in, 7-11
  hashing function for, 35-41
  human-selected, 9-11
  in identification system context, 11
  most popular, 3
  one-time passwords, 103-106
  peppering, 34
  poor choices for, 3
  randomly selected, 8
  removing, for self-signed certificates, 143
  salting, 32-34
  secure hash generation for, 41
  security questions, 14
  validating against a hashed value, 40-41
password attacks
  brute force attacks, 20-22
  CAPTCHA creation with reCAPTCHA, 22-28
  dictionary attacks, 28
  peppering to prevent, 34
  rainbow tables, 30-32
  reverse lookup tables, 29
  salting to prevent, 32-34
  vectors, 20-32
password entropy, 7
  (see also entropy)
password fatigue, 6
PayPal, Node and, 132
PBKDF2 (Password-Based Key Derivation Function 2), 12, 37
people, as weakest link in security chain, 5-7
peppering, 34
persistent XSS, 125
phishing, 20, 67
phone numbers, for thin identity, 45

plug-ins
  browser fingerprinting, 51
  JavaScript library for plug-in information, 51
POST requests
  self-signed certificates, 145-146
  two-factor authentication, 108-112
  XSS protection, 126
private key, removing password/encryption for self-signed certificates, 143
public/private key encryption (see asynchronous cryptography)

R

rainbow tables, 21, 30-32
random salt, 33
randomBytes(…) method, 33
randomly-selected passwords, entropy in, 8
reCAPTCHA, 22-28
reduction function, 30
reflected XSS, 125
Refresh Tokens
  client-side OAuth 2.0, 94
  lifetime management, 75-78, 76
  OAuth 2.0, 70
  using, 81
rejectUnauthorized: false option, 148
Resource Owner Password Credentials Grant, 95
resource requests, OAuth 2.0, 78-80
response object, 82
retina scanning, 114
reverse lookup tables, 29
RSA (Rivest-Shamir-Adleman) key, 142
RSA Tokens, 103

S

salt/salting, 32-34
  (see also hashing function)
  appropriate length, 34
  dictionary attack prevention, 29
  peppering vs., 34
  rainbow table attack prevention, 31
  random generation, 33
  reuse, 33
  storage, 34
  synchronous generation, 33
scope parameter, 88, 97
scope, of client, 74

screen resolution, for browser fingerprinting, 51
scrypt, 13, 38
Secure Hash Algorithm (see SHA entries)
Secure Sockets Layer (see SSL)
security
    for existing systems, 12-13
    humans as weakest link, 5-7
    usability vs., 4
security layering, 119
security models, problems with current, 1-5
security modules
    Helmet, 133
    Lusca, 132
security questions, 14
self-signed certificates, 141-148
    certificate setup, 142-144
    error from using in production, 141
    marking secure requests to server, 146-148
    removing key encryption, 143
    server setup, 144-148
server
    adding OpenID Connect functionality to, 86-91
    database setup for OAuth 2.0, 69-86
    for OAuth 2.0, 68-91
    secure requests with self-signed certificates, 146-148
    setup for self-signed certificates, 144-146
session(s)
    best practices for, 124
    cookies, 120
    defined, 121
    Express and, 121-125
    management with OpenID Connect, 91
    securing, 119-125
    types of, 120
SHA-1, 13
SHA-2, 13, 122
SHA-256, 122
Shannon Entropy, 9
ShoCard, 118
shopping cart abandonment, 4
short message service (SMS) verification code (see SMS verification code)
single sign-on (SSO), 6
Slack
    mobile sign-in flow, 104
    security breach, 5

Smart Lock, 46
smart phones, device fingerprinting for, 54
SMS (short message service) verification code
    sending, 109
    validating, 110
social engineering
    defined, 20
    encryption and, 13
social identity, 44
social media, logins for, 58
SSL (Secure Sockets Layer), 137-148
    certificate validation types and authorities, 139-141
    domain validation, 139
    extended validation, 140
    organization validation, 139
    self-signed certificates, 141-148
SSO (single sign-on), 6
synchronous (symmetric) cryptography, 158-169
    advantages of, 168
    AES with CTR encryption, 164
    AES with GCM encryption, 166-168
    block cipher modes of operation, 162-164
    disadvantages of, 169
    initialization vector, 159
    padding, 160
    uses of, 169

T

tablets, device fingerprinting for, 54
text messages, for OTPs, 103
thin identity, 45
three-legged OAuth, 59
time zone, for browser fingerprinting, 51
TLS (Transport Layer Security), 138
    (see also SSL)
Token Endpoint, 89
tokens, 70
    (see also specific tokens, e.g.: Access Tokens)
    endpoint modification with OpenID Connect, 89
    handling lifetime of, 75-78
    OAuth 2.0 Access Tokens, 70
    OAuth 2.0 Refresh Tokens, 70
    UUIDs for OAuth 2.0, 70-72
TouchID, 113
Transport Layer Security (TLS), 138

(see also SSL)
trust zones, 46-47
Twilio, 106
Twitter
    Digits service, 45
    hybrid OAuth implementation, 63
two-factor authentication (2FA), 102-112
    Authy, 106-112
    one-time passwords, 103-106
two-legged OAuth, 59

U

U2F (Universal 2nd Factor) standard, 116
UAF (Universal Authentication Framework)
    protocol, 116
ursa package, 152-156
usability, security vs., 4
user agent, browser details from, 50
user, as weakest link in security chain, 5-7
UserInfo endpoint, 66, 91
username
    biometrics as alternative to, 112
    in context of identification system, 11
UUIDs (Universal Unique Identifiers), 70-72

V

vein recognition, 115

W

web applications, hardening, 119-135
    CSRF attacks, 130-132
    handling XSS, 125-130
    Node modules, 132-134
    securing sessions, 119-125
    various mitigation techniques, 134
WebKit, XSS Auditor and, 128

X

X-XSS-Protection header, 129
XSS (cross-site scripting)
    circumventing XSS Auditor, 128-130
    handling, 125-130
    protection mechanism testing, 126-130
    token storage, 94
    types of, 125
XSS Auditor, 128-130

Y

Yahoo!, one-time-only passwords for, 45

About the Authors

Jonathan LeBlanc is an Emmy award-winning software engineer, technical author, and the Head of Global Developer Advocacy for PayPal. Jonathan specializes in identity, authorization, and security; hardware-to-web communications; and data mining techniques—all with a focus towards human and device interconnectivity.

Tim Messerschmidt is Program Manager of Developer Relations at Google, leading the Germany, Austria, and Switzerland (DACH) region. Prior to joining Google, he headed up PayPal's and Braintree's Developer Evangelism teams across Europe, Middle East, and Africa (EMEA) and the Asia-Pacific (APAC) region.

Colophon

The fish on the cover of *Identity and Data Security for Web Development* is a long-tail seamoth (*Pegasus volitans*) also known as the batfish, sea dragon, or dragonfish. They are covered with bony plates arranged in concentric rings and their pectoral fins are large and winglike. Seamoths live in shallow coastal waters with beds of seagrass or seaweed and sandy or silty bottoms.

Most seamoths measure 5 inches (13 cm) but the long-tail seamoth measures 7 inches (18 cm). Despite their name, the large fin muscles of a seamoth are not strong enough for flapping flight. The fins are most useful to change a predator's view, quickly expanding to add width and depth to a seemingly nondescript fish. The mouth is situated on the underside of a long snout, which indicates seamoths are bottom feeders; feasting on minuscule animals that live among the grains of sand. They are poor swimmers and do not travel far, yet are widely dispersed across oceans because their larvae are carried thousands of miles by ocean currents as part of the plankton. The seamoths have dispersed themselves throughout the coastal waters of the southern Pacific and Indian Oceans all the way to South Africa. They cannot survive the cold barrier in the sea off the Cape of Good Hope, so they have yet to reach the Atlantic Ocean.

Many of the animals on O'Reilly covers are endangered; all of them are important to the world. To learn more about how you can help, go to *animals.oreilly.com*.

The cover image is from *Wood's Natural History*. The cover fonts are URW Typewriter and Guardian Sans. The text font is Adobe Minion Pro; the heading font is Adobe Myriad Condensed; and the code font is Dalton Maag's Ubuntu Mono.

Have it your way.

Get even more for your money.

Join the O'Reilly Community, and register the O'Reilly books you own. It's free, and you'll get:

- $4.99 ebook upgrade offer
- 40% upgrade offer on O'Reilly print books
- Membership discounts on books and events
- Free lifetime updates to ebooks and videos
- Multiple ebook formats, DRM FREE
- Participation in the O'Reilly community
- Newsletters
- Account management
- 100% Satisfaction Guarantee

Signing up is easy:

1. Go to: oreilly.com/go/register
2. Create an O'Reilly login.
3. Provide your address.
4. Register your books.

Note: English-language books only

To order books online:
oreilly.com/store

For questions about products or an order:
orders@oreilly.com

To sign up to get topic-specific email announcements and/or news about upcoming books, conferences, special offers, and new technologies:
elists@oreilly.com

For technical questions about book content:
booktech@oreilly.com

To submit new book proposals to our editors:
proposals@oreilly.com

O'Reilly books are available in multiple DRM-free ebook formats. For more information:
oreilly.com/ebooks